Mediterranean Diet

The Ultimate Guide and Cookbook for Lasting Weight Loss

Emma Moore

Table of Contents

MEDITERRANEAN DIET FOR BEGINNERS

(BOOK 1)
Introduction

Congratulations for viewing this Book:

"Mediterranean Diet for Beginners: The Complete Guide to Mediterranean Lifestyle Featuring Healthy Recipes and a 7-Day Meal Plan to Kick-Start Your Weight Loss".

It is a guide that aims at emphasizing on plant-based foods. These foods include vegetables, legumes, whole grains, nuts, and much more.

In addition to discussing primarily plant foods, this book will demonstrate how butter can be replaced with natural healthy fats. Such fats are the canola oil and the popular olive oil. A lot more will be deliberated in this informative book including the use of spices and herbs to flavor foods instead of using salt.

There is nothing that fulfills the heart of most people than having a weight loss meal plan that does not require you to sacrifice your taste buds. Your meals will be healthy and still comprise enjoyable and diverse tastes. The Mediterranean diet for starters combines savory recipes and meal plans that guide you every time you desire to have that sumptuous meal. It is the only reference for anyone who wishes to follow the Mediterranean diet.

Intensive research has been done while writing this book. The sources that have been used to develop this manuscript are reliable and approved. Prior to publishing this book, a lot of vetting was carried out to avoid compromising the content. As a result, be confident with the knowledge you gain from reading this eBook. Do not be afraid to use the information found here to better your health. However, you can seek professional guidance when necessary. You can conduct personal research as well in case you find some information limiting. It won't cost a dime but will build your knowledge on the subject. Remember, it is powerful to be more knowledgeable.

The diet is considered to be one of the healthiest meal plans around the world. The reason placed behind this notion is that the diet offers a comprehensive guide to healthy eating. The foods are freshly prepared and organic keeping in mind the well-being of the reader. So, read on!

History and Theory

The Mediterranean diet was a sensational re-discovery by Ancel Keys, a world-renowned nutritionist. The finding was made in the sixties as an improvement to the ancient diet. As the name suggests, the popular and healthy Mediterranean diet consists of two words, 'Mediterranean' and 'Diet.' Let's examine the two words so that you can have a crystal-clear understanding of what you will be applying in your meals.

Mediterranean: There is a sea that is between Africa, Asia, and Europe. The sea is named the Mediterranean. From its west, it has a natural entry from the huge Atlantic Ocean, and from its East, it has a manmade exit. The exit is in the direction of the Red Sea. The Latins were the first ones to name the sea in the third century. They first named it Mare Mediterranean, which means the sea that is between two continents. In the Latin language, Mare merely means the sea.

The Mediterranean diet was established by the countries that surround the Mediterranean Sea. In these countries, olive trees and fruits grew in abundance. They grew for four seasons in a row. The mild climatic conditions in the Mediterranean region caused abundance. Since fishing was the major occupation within the region, people came up with a diet that comprised of fish and fruits. It became a diet that was a reference to many, and hence, it was named the Mediterranean diet. Additionally, there were the Mediterranean herbs that were used for cooking and medicinal purposes as well.

Diet: In normal circumstances, the word diet is associated with negativity, as opposed to its original meaning as you will find out. Presumably, you know the word to express limitation, and in our case, limited food. In the event that one adds weight, there is a pathological theory that you have accumulated fats in your body. It could be true, and if it were

3

true, you get statements that you should diet. However, this is not so with the Mediterranean diet.

Diet is a Greek word that means a way of living. It is allied to the broad spectrum of people's lifestyles, their work, social environment, sleep, social activities, place of residence, and a lot more. In ancient Greek, the way of life was commonly dictated by god Dias. He dictated on the food to eat, where and when work, where to stay and even sleep! So, when you decide to follow the Mediterranean diet, your commitment should get even stronger, if theory and history is anything to go by.

You now realize that the word 'diet' has been an overly overstated affair. By following the Mediterranean diet, you do not only lose weight, but you adopt a healthy eating lifestyle that will also help you avoid lifestyle diseases caused by unhealthy eating.

Chapter 1: Comparison of American Lifestyle and Other Famous Diets

Complete package for beginners on dieting

It is wise to start out the Mediterranean diet by selecting whole foods rather than processed foods. As much as you enjoy a little tipple of sugary drinks from time to time, it is highly advisable to avoid them or limit their intake. Whether you are doing your outdoor chores or traveling, ensure healthy foods are readily available. While buying foods, use popular America's 'outer ring' method. Currently, critics put it as the best technique for beginners on dieting. Try 'nuts for nuts' or 'seeds for seeds' during your shopping spree. It is also recommended to take fish portions regularly. Also, consider using full grain flour while preparing your baking recipes. Finally, you might be the 'boozy brunch' type of a person when it comes to meals, this time around, consider taking food in small portions.

Dieting

Dieting - sounds familiar, especially for the ladies who fight to have that appealing body shape, right? Most people, more so women, find a lot of confidence from having slim and healthy bodies as opposed to being overweight. Dieting is the exercise of taking food in a more regulated or monitored style. The reason behind regulated dieting is to maintain healthy body weight as well as avoid the onset of lifestyle diseases associated with obesity. There are also medicinal reasons for a restricted diet; to treat and prevent lifestyle diseases such as type 2 diabetes, cardiovascular diseases, and depression among others. A combination of a healthy meal plan with regulated physical activity helps in preventing these diseases, and in cases where a person is already suffering from obesity or cardiovascular diseases, it helps in their treatment.

Sure, you can shed that weight fast. Numerous fads diets around America help to cut those pounds fast, but they will leave you feeling deprived and as hungry as a desert viper. The good news is that the Mediterranean diet never leaves you 'gasping' for more food as if it were air. The Mediterranean diet is not a fad diet promising miracles overnight but it is a healthier way of eating that promises long-term benefits to your health.

Tips to get you started on dieting

- Never skip meals; seek for alternative meal plans that match the diet plan.
- Do not get too rigid on certain foods, but rather, be flexible while preparing the recipes.
- Drink water 1 hour or 30 minutes prior to your meals.
- Eat every time you experience a spike of hunger.
- Don't mix snacks and food.
- For quick and easy digestion, use wine.
- Don't eat any processed food; instead, stick to whole unprocessed foods only.
- Exercise regularly, with the help of a certified instructor.
- Motivate yourself through positive self-talk.
- Keep on checking your calorie levels to ensure that they are improving.
- Check your weight regularly.

In most parts of the world, there are different types of diets when it comes to meal planning. Some are based on theories and scientific research while others are based on traditional cultures and belief systems. This section will be comparing an American diet which in this case is the Mediterranean diet from other diets found in the rest of the world and what makes them special altogether.

of them are at a level that needs medical attention through undergoing weight loss surgery.

3. Exercise tip (don't engage in any physical activity if you are not willing to stick to the diet as well – they go hand-in-hand).
4. The best approach to the diet is through coaching and training.
5. The quickest exercises that proved to work faster included the Stairmaster, boat rowing, and doing tiresome jobs.

Critics

Recently, it has been argued that through people's testimonials, most of those that tried this diet ended up gaining more weight. Other reviews also showed that a couple of them maintained the same weight.

Atkins Diet

Talk of evolutions and popularity; this is one of the most popular diets that even some American celebrities adore. The diet focuses on low fats through restriction of carbs in the body. The restriction is encouraged in order to allow the body to store food instead of just processing food all the times. According to the reviews by a lot of people who have been on this diet, it is the best diet for losing weight and works faster. The restriction of carbs comes in handy to curb chronic and heart diseases. These diseases majorly affect overweight or obese people. So, if you sometimes experience a spike in your blood pressure, it's time you engage the Atkins diet.

How to get started with the Atkins diet

Atkins diet is the best diet for beginners; this is according to recent research by the American health department.

Below are7 simple ways on how you can get started with this diet.

1. Set goals

   Set achievable goals. To attain a successful Atkins diet program, it essential to set reasonable goals. Set goals that you are sure you will achieve within a stipulated time frame, and those that match your diet budget as well. Goals will keep you motivated while still giving you a reason to work towards your objective.

2. Know your meal plan

   When you are ready with your goals, determine which Atkins diet plan is right for you. It could be the Atkins 20 or the Atkins 40. For Atkins 20, you will begin with the induction part. In this part, you will shift your body from burning carbs to burning fats. You will take 20grams of carbs per day.

   For the Atkins 40, your net carb intake will be an average of 40grams per day. As you approach your goals, you will definitely need to increase your carb intake appropriately. This gradual adjustment helps you maintain your momentum of weight loss.

3. Follow the approved foods

   Approved foods are those that are recommended by the doctor. The diet emphasizes people to follow the doctor's guideline before starting on the Atkins meal plan. This will enable them to avoid diseases that might follow because of not sticking to the doctor's advice. The plan also advocates that the daily carb intake is not exceeded at any one time.

4. Follow the recipes

Recipes are very important and very effective. Meals only work well when proper channels are followed. One slight mistake might spoil the whole meal at the end. Following a recipe to the latter will save you a lot of time. Secondly, you will save on your budget and reverted meals will be eliminated. Third, and most importantly, you will maintain the net carb intake. Finally, you will not miss out on anything, that's very fulfilling for any beginner.

5. Snack

Snacks are also very important when it comes to health. They may appear simple on the menu, but the kind of effect they have on the body is very high. Some of the snacks include natural yogurt, raspberry, and fruits. Fruits are known for having a lot of vitamins for the body like vitamin B2 and vitamin C which help in improving night vision. Fruits are what you are advised to eat a lot. Even if it is 3 apples a day, it would do just fine.

6. Eat a lot of fat

Atkins diet does not come with a limitation to fat consumption. Instead, you are advised to eat foods rich in fats. The concept here is that when you want to lose weight faster, it gives the body enough room to gain muscle as you exercise.

7. Get motivation

The best way to getting stellar results while in the diet is by making sure that you surround yourself with people with the same goals. Get yourself friends who will tell you it is time to go and exercise, go on a road trip, and do a little hike. Get friends who will see you sitting in the house, and they will quickly assign you home chores to get you on the right shape. Good friends and family will not get you off your meal plan, but they will make sure to help you even if it means that they will be the ones to cook for you at times.

What to consider on your diet when on a low-carb diet

There are three foods to consider when you are on a low-carb diet. They are very effective for the individual.

- Vegetables
- Cheese
- Eggs

In as much as we focus on what to eat on low-carb, we should also not forget what not to put in the mouth when on the diet.

- Bread
- Candy
- Saturated Fats
- Fish
- Donuts
- Fruits
- Meat

Wine is very important to drink when on a low-carb diet. Wine, in this case, is considered very useful when it comes to digestion of food. Other drinks you can try out also are whiskey and a little beer, but not more than half glass at the end of the day. Tea and coffee are not recommended. They should be avoided at all costs.

Benefits of the Atkins Diet

1. The diet improves and nourishes the skin tone; it makes the skin appear more smooth and light.

Cons

1. Low protein consumption

    The diet encourages low protein consumption; this poses as an anomaly. Your body needs protein to repair tissues and build them as well. Proteins are used to make hormones, enzymes, and other critical body chemicals. Blood, cartilage, skin,and bones are also developed through proteins. So, its deficiency is quite harmful.

2. Limited diet

    The worst thing about this diet is that the diet is very limiting as it has a lot of stringent rules. Some measures are helpful though, but others only bring loss and exposure to diseases.

3. Hard to maintain

    Macrobiotic diet might be good but is also very hard to maintain. A person considering starting on this diet is one with no rush when it comes to cooking. The diet is hard to maintain because almost all the foods are prepared from scratch and may take a lot of time before the food is finally cooked and ready for eating. This means you might be tempted to opt to choose something else to cook instead of sticking to the meal plan of the macrobiotic diet.

How to get started with the macrobiotic diet

Being a very sensitive diet, the first step is to consider your reasons behind following the diet. Place some value on the diet before you start. Consider the benefits versus the flaws. Such a step will help you look forward to the end result.

The next step is to approach a doctor for proper guidelines especially if you might be suffering from any diseases in order to know the way forward. Get the go-ahead from a certified doctor who will parade your bodily conveniences to the diet. Doctors make important contributions in selecting the best diet that suits you.

The third step to take is to make sure that you do not have any plastic utensils in the kitchen for cooking or serving, you should clear all of them in case they are there. This concept is related to macro science, which partly studies the effects of plastics materials in your body, especially when they are hot.

The fourth step is to check and ensure that you are not using the microwave. Another concept associated with macro science. The last step is to make sure that your mind is set and ready to commit to the diet to the fullest without any hesitations. A settled mind has the advantage of achieving the set goals.

Mediterranean diet versus a macrobiotic diet

Diet is a very basic topic when it comes to food and nutrition. It comes with a lot of various meal plans that have evolved over the years. Some diets have almost everything in common. Studies have shown that the more the diets increased, the more people came up with their own fad diets. It reached a point where the scientists decided to take over and make researches on these diets to come up with the best guide to give people for their meal plan.

The Mediterranean diet and macrobiotic diet are the best choices and have a lot of commonalities. Mediterranean diet is majorly basedonseafood and very popular among the Italians. The macrobiotic diet is based on a system which is used to discover the right choice of nutrients for people to have.

Difference

The Mediterranean diet is based on traditional foods while the macrobiotic diet is based on the civilized people. These foods are very natural and are not man-made. They do not involve any processing. They come from animals and plants. Such foods include, and not limited to, fish, chicken, pork, meat, fruits, whole grains, and much more. Macrobiotic diet food choices are influenced greatly by how civilized people are. The system was introduced for people to eat according to their class level.

The Mediterranean diet is a lifestyle diet while the macrobiotic diet attempts to be mindful at discovering the patterns of healthy living. This implies that with the Mediterranean diet, people eat naturally without any stringent rules or limitations. In a nutshell, their eating habits are part of them. However, with the macrobiotic diet, people follow it because of health reasons.

The macrobiotic diet is based on a daily pyramid while the Mediterranean diet is based on a lifetime choice. This means that on the macrobiotic diet, people are limited to what they should eat based on daily consumption while for people on a Mediterranean diet, there are no rules.

Everything You Need To Know About Obesity As A Beginner: Complete Guide

Obesity

Obesity is a medical condition that is attached too much fat in the body, leading to problems like hypertension, type 2 diabetes, and in some instances, depression. There are two levels of obesity when it comes to dieting and science. There are the medium-size obesity and overweight-obesity. The two are handled in different ways as they are not the same. The medium-size obesity is controlled by proper dieting, by making sure you have followed theproper meal plan every day. Also, the condition is regulated by engaging in a lot of physical exercises to maintain the body.

Overweight obesity is the worst condition that would ever happen to a person. It is the state that no amount of dieting or any exercises can help you get back to your natural body. The only cause of action is seeking medical help which involves going for surgery. An overweight surgery has a lot of medical procedures before you are released from the hospital. It also comes with it a handful of measures that you must grit to stick with them. The most grueling part is the limitations to food. Coincidentally, you are cautionedagainstfoods that you crave for such as candy, fizzy drinks, fast foods among others.

Obesity is stimulated by the fact that these people over eat unhealthy foods and don't do any exercise for their bodies or even taking part in any housework chores. They are, therefore, advised to do regular exercise to return to a manageable weight. Simple exercises can kick start your journey to regular body weight. An exercise such as walking around every day after having your meals is quite effective as a beginner. Body stretches are also helpful to avoid swollen knees and painful joints.

Below are some effects of what comes after you reach obesity level.

- You will start experiencing breathing problems and the heart pumps faster.
- A lot of sweating in the body even without necessarily engaging in any activity.
- Problems with sleeping because of regular snoring with a big awful sound.
- Body pains all over because the bones are weak and can't do much
- Urge for water will be more than you were used to as the body tends to dehydrate more.
- Waking up tired all the time even after doing very simple tasks.
- Your self-esteem will drastically go down because of encountering criticism from people while others keep on staring at you.
- Isolating yourself from other people and getting yourself eating all alone in a corner.
- Regular visits to the toilet.

Obesity in children

When you are obese, you are all the things people are except an abnormal weight, a few pounds heavier. The consequences of premature aging, dramatic physical changes, and much more. Children tend to hide from life and repress the condition. In

America alone, the numbers of overweight children have doubled in recent years. Obesity is known to affect children more than it affects adults.

There are several factors that cause obesity in children. They include family eating habits, unhealthy food choices, and zero physical exercises. Most likely, overweight children will become obese adults. What causes obesity? Simple. If you take in more food than you use, the extra energy will be stored as fat. The accumulated fat is what is termed as obesity.

Let's analyze the factors that cause obesity in brief.

- Food Choices – Taking in sugary foods and those with high fats.
- Physical Activities – Lack of physical bodily activities causes fats not to burn out.
- Sedentary Pursuits – excessive television watching, playing computer and electronic games rather than physical activities. On average, American children watch television for three to four hours a day.
- Overweight Parents – The eating patterns of parents can absolutely have a significant influence on the eating habits of their children. Overweight Parents can be less concerned about the weight of their children, be it healthy or unhealthy.
- Genetics – Gene disorders trick the body hormones to develop unnecessary fats.

Overweight children are vulnerable to bitter criticism. As a result, bullying ensues both in schools and at home.

Bullying by Obese Children

The table changes at times and becomes the opposite of the expectation. How? You may ask. Obese children take advantage of their situations because, at this moment, they know that they are bigger. Now that they are big-bodied, unlike when they were small, they turn their rage on kids who used to bully them, who now apparently, appear smaller. At this level, they feel very masculine, and truly they are, they start bullying others as a means of revenge. The sad news is that they are more aggressive than those bullies who used to bully them.

Bullying by obese children grows by the day; they tend to eat more and more in order to have big bodies to fight and bully the other kids in school. Only, instead of getting better health-wise, their health continues heading south.

How to Handle Bullying

The truth is, handling bullying is quite an uphill task. However, a bully can get power to the extent you only allow them to get. The biblical story of Goliath and the boy David is an excellent example of the feeble vanquishing the strong. Nonetheless, it is not as easy as it sounds. There is a genius path you need to follow while handling bullying.

1. Be Confident – Win bullies with firm, strong, and courteous demeanor.
2. Stay Connected – Maintain connections with true supportive adults and friends. Bullies won't see you lonely and powerless.
3. Set Limits – Remain firm while still being professional and polite. The bully should not get beneath your skin.
4. Act Quickly but Consistently – To prevent the bully's aggression from worsening, report to an adult immediately, follow the routine always.
5. Use unemotional Language – Bitter exchange of words with abully gives them a sense of power they are seeking.
6. Strike while the cobra lays low - Step back for a little while, you will get a solid solution when the heads are cool.

Can bullies change for the better?

Approaching bullies are very easy. They might not change immediately, but when approached the right way, they will eventually change for the better.

1. Take action

   As a parent, it is very important to make sure that you don't take bullying lightly. The consequences of bullying may become worse in due course. Take your time, approach the child and show them the detriments of bullying. The trick is, respond promptly without getting hostile.

2. Set an example

   It is very important to watch your ways all the time because the child will follow what you are doing. Be careful how you approach your situations like anger. Learn to manage it, not overreacting to situations. This will make it very easy for the child to change. Good parents don't just love their children, they give them the best when growing up, and setting a good example is in the list for that.

3. Control media exposure for your child

   Ensure that your child listens and watches relevant things from the media. Don't let your child watch movies that will only encourage him to instigate fights when he goes back to school the next day.

4. Seek professional help

When you notice that the situation is getting out of hand, ensure that you go and seek external help from other parents with the experience. You will surely return home with one or two methods on how to handle the situation. Seeking professional intervention is the best way forward. It helps to make sure that you handle the situation in the correct way.Stay consistent in the method you decide to adapt. You can as well combine several techniques that are freely available online.

Chapter 2: HowThe Mediterranean Lifestyle Can Improve Your Health

Every diet has an end result attached to it, the Mediterranean diet is no exception, and it was also started with the purpose of improving health for people. Below are some of the reasons why you should definitely try the Mediterranean diet.

1. Preserves memory and cognitive decline
2. Reduces the risk of heart diseases
3. Strengthens bones
4. Improves blood sugar levels
5. Fights depression
6. Protect against cancer

A) Preserve the memory and cognitive decline

Mediterranean diet has been proven to help in preserving memory and cognitive decline especially when it comes to adults. Some of these motivators are believed to be rich in omega 3 and omega 6, like fish and extra olive oil. Researchers who analyzed this theory came to conclude that the results were more effective especially to those who keenly followed the diet without going out of the way. They also concluded that, for cognitive decline, it was more effective with those who did not engage in excessive alcohol intake or even smoking. It also works pretty effectively with the old people who stuck well with medications given to them.

b) Reduce the risk of heart diseases

Compared to the United States, the prevalence of heart diseases in the Mediterranean countries is lower. The concept is surely attributed to the great practice of the

e) Protect against cancer

Some or most cancers are brought about by overweight or obese conditions. Others such as breast cancer are greatly influenced by what the person eats. For breast cancer,some microorganisms grow around the breast and become malignant. The Mediterranean diet is very important because it is through it that the bacteria (microorganisms) that grows and spreads around the breast gets to be killed.

Fiber is known to be a preventive measure of cancer-related diseases. Studies on the Mediterranean diet discovered that, since the people on this diet eat a lot of vegetables and fruits, the rate of being diagnosed with cancer is low.

f) Lasting Agility

All the nutrients comprised in the Mediterranean diet including the vitamins and the minerals, ensure that the risk of having muscle weakness is reduced at a bigger percentage. These substances also cater for any other matters in the body that may increase frailty. As a matter of fact, studies show that the risks reduce by a whopping 70%. Therefore, by taking lots of vegetables, fruits, lean proteins, and healthy fats, while engaging in physical activity, you maintain a healthy weight, hence, are also assured of lasting agility.

g) The Diet delays the onset of Alzheimer's Disease

Alzheimer's disease also known as Dementia is controlled through this type of nutritional plan. The diet improves your cholesterol levels, blood sugar levels, plus the entire blood vessels in your body. Through time, health practitioners have encouraged patients to adopt eating habits that are in line with the Mediterranean Diet. It is an effort to address cognitive conditions and dementia.

h) The Mediterranean Lifestyle Controls the Risk of getting Parkinson's Disease
Almost by half, the diet reduces the risk of being diagnosed with Parkinson's disease. What causes Parkinson's disease? It is when your body undergoes the oxidative stress process. The process causes huge damage to the cells leading to developing degenerative diseases such as Parkinson's disease.

When you consume a lot of antioxidants which can only be drawn from seafood dishes, vegetables, fruits, and healthy fats, your body counters the process of oxidative stress.

There are environmental factors that trigger these types of diseases, but researches are still underway. These researches are checking on the role played by nutrition in neuro degeneration and neuro protection. In the meantime, the Mediterranean diet has proved to counter this disease if followed to the brim.

i) Healthy Weight Loss

Unlike so many other restrictive diets, the Mediterranean diet helps you shed weight effectively. Reasons being that you can be able to maintain the diet in the long term without so much stress. It has your favorite selection of foods that are readily available and affordable. Without realizing it,you will notice that you have lost a significant amount of weight in the long run. With this diet, you will still feel satiated and perhaps not be consciously aware that you are still under the diet.

Nonetheless, it is not as easy as it seems, but it is still the most manageable diet you will ever have. You are required to follow the diet for not less than six months, or even for a lifetime. For significant results of the meal plan, check on your food portions. Small amounts of crabs and breads will do, however, if you are not careful with the amounts, you might compromise your goals of losing that unwanted weight. It is also prudent to engage in regular physical exercises for you to get to that stellar physic.

j) The Diet Fights Inflammations

Intense research has been conducted to investigate the role of the nutritional plan on inflammation biomarkers. The study shows that the diet can mitigate and control these markers. By extension, the diet controls inflammation inside the body as well as preventing massive destruction of cells that is caused by chronic inflammation.

You already know that foods found on Mediterranean diet contain a lot of antioxidants. Inflammation is caused by exposing your body to oxidative stress; apparently, the diet will counter this process.

k) Improved Fertility

Studies on 500 women revealed that those who took plenty of vegetables, whole grains, fruits,and fish increased their fertility.

Chapter 3: How The Mediterranean Diet Improves Sexual Health

As you can vividly see now, the Mediterranean diet has significant effects on your health. These effects can either be long-term or short-term. Your health encompasses your entire well-being, your fitness, your psychology, and (this one you knew I had to mention) your sex life.

Did you know that food can boost your sexual activity? The truth is that most people don't know this; in fact, they think that sexual performance is very normal and can happen any time they want. Well, that might be true naturally, but when science is involved, the sex drive is triggered by what the body is fed on and not just a natural thing.

The best thing about the Mediterranean diet is the fact that it focuses on freshly cooked food and highly discourages processed food. Most people who are used to processed foods have a low sex drive because the foods that they eat are just for hunger satisfaction and not a balanced diet that focuses on the health of an individual. Currently, the Mediterranean diet is rated one of the best fitness diets among the rest as it focuses mainly on health fitness of an individual, as well as their sexual health.

To most people, sexual drive is just a natural thing, but the truth is that it is not just a natural thing, it is depended on a lot of factors in the body. For instance, when it comes to the sex drive, the body depends on factors like body fitness, whether you are overweight or not. If the body is overweight or obese, that is a retrogressive factor. This is because the accumulated fats Sexual drive is very low because the sexual organs do not receive the expected blood flow. Poor sexual performance is inevitable to obese people. Occasionally, these people get embarrassed, and the obvious result is for the relationship to start fraying away.

Did you know that diabetes affects sex drive? Probably, since you are a beginner in dieting, you don't. Well, diabetes affects sexual performance at a very high rate. The Mediterranean diet is important especially because it helps in fighting diabetes and making the body stronger.

Studies have proved that your sexual health can be improved by eating well and engaging in physical activities. The Mediterranean diet takes all these into account. Eating healthier foods will result in better sex life, and is usually expected with this kind of a diet. All components of the diet have a critical effect on your body, but there are those nutrients that have an effect on your sexual life.

Since the cave days, pomegranate has been considered as a love fruit. The fruit's juice has magnificent antioxidant qualities. These qualities assist in decreasing arterial plaque. This enhances blood circulation and flow throughout the entire body. To the penis, this improves its erection duration as well as its hardness.

Perhaps, you might be wondering, what about the popular myth about nuts and their role in sexual health. First, it is not a myth, it is a fact that nuts improve sex life. Oily nuts, such as the walnuts, have a tremendous effect on enhanced sexual drive. Couples who follow the Mediterranean diet consistently enjoy sexual pleasure more than those who don't. Their desire for sex is increased, they are aroused regularly, and hit the orgasm button frequently.

The Med diet consists of olive oil as part of the meal plan. The oil has been known to improve sexual health for both women and men across the globe. Olive oil has high levels of antioxidants. These antioxidants curb the process of artery clogging. When the arteries are freely opened up, blood flows effectively,and this triggers a prolonged erection. Additionally, a more fascinating fact about olive oil is that it slows down aging, and the longevity of sex life is experienced for couples.

As of now, you already know that the Mediterranean diet reduces cholesterol levels. When these levels are low, blood flow is increased in every part of the body including the male reproductive organ. As a result, the erectile capacity is enhanced as well. By extension, you can note that the testosterone levels are increased through the Med diet, hence enhancing one's sex life. The diet also heightens the sexual desire for women who follow it as opposed to those that don't.

Medically, Med Diet is not closely related to fertility. Nonetheless, women who are under medical treatment for fertility and still follow the diet are prone to getting pregnant than those who are not under the diet. This improved fertility rate is attached to the high consumption of fish, vegetable oil, and vegetables.

Your eyebrows will definitely rise when you read the following fact. According to research that was conducted by universities in America, a child's sex is related to what the mother ate during the first few months before conception. The study was done after it was discovered that the birth of boys had declined over the past several years as compared to the birth of girls. The extensive research focused on what the mothers ate. Women who were obese gave birth to boys, implying that they took in more fats. You would expect what followed, women started having more cereals, especially for breakfast, and alas! They gave birth to baby boys.

5 Types of Foods that will boost Your Sex Drive

A recent study on women revealed the importance of the Med Diet. It showed that the diet helped improve scores on the FSFI or the female sexual function index. Generally, the diet comprises of fruits, whole grains, vegetables, nuts,and olive oil. A good number of women in this study mentioned that they never missed the following foods in their diet as much as they seldom skipped some other foods.

1. Avocado

   In ancient times, Spanish priests restricted the Aztecs from having avocados in their meals. There was a concept that the fruit acted as a sex booster. In recent times, science has proven the notion right. The fruit contains folic acid as well as potassium. These two elements support energy or stamina. So, it is true, the priests were correct.

2. Wild Salmon

   The wild salmon has the popular omega 3 fats. The fatty acids enhance vascular health and support blood circulation for sexual function. As a result, the flow of blood to the brain is increased, which in turn, supports mental feelings and relaxation. When the mind is at ease, you are ready to roll in the grass.

3. Red Wine

   So far, you have seen the benefits that come along with having a slight tipple of red wine. Back in 2009, there was a hilarious but very educative study on three types of women, Italian women to be precise. They were the moderate wine takers, tee totalers, and serious alcohol consumers. The moderate type of women scored best on the FSFI. The FSFI indicated satisfaction, pain, arousal, desire, orgasm, and lubrication.

4. Dark Chocolate

No, don't think about that, the style and the huge amounts chocolate is consumed in America, the sweet tasty candy; a disaster to the hormones, especially libido. Think about dark chocolate and eliminate or reduce sugar content in your diet. Dark chocolate enhances sexual function and desire, and its sugar level is balanced.

5. Tomatoes

True, you can label it as natural Viagra, if you like. It contains strong antioxidants, more powerful than the popular beta-carotene. Tomatoes comprise of an element known as Lycopene. The substance eases the blood vessels and thus improves blood circulation. To attain high Lycopene content, ensure the tomatoes you buy are free from any chemical processing. Any chemical processing increases oxidation, and as a result, nutrients are lost at a high percentage.

Here is a little mind shaker. The Mediterranean lifestyle does not only come as a deterrent to lifestyle diseases in the future but helps you enjoy life and its pleasures for now, in particular, a pleasant sex life. Also, it comes as a new school of health, whereby, you can come out of a health practitioner's office with instructions, not about tablets, but a prescription for red wine, salmon, tomatoes, avocados, and the sumptuous dark chocolate!

Mediterranean Diet is better than Viagra

Recently, the University of Athens conducted passionate research and found out that nine tablespoons of olive oil per week could work better than the popular Viagra or sometimes referred to as Sildenafil. You already know that olive oil is part

40

of the Med Diet. According to the study, the prescription improved erectile dysfunction by an amazing forty percent. You can get this revelation from the journal 'Circulation.' So, it is sensible to include olive oil in your daily meals.

Apart from the fact that olive oil enhances blood circulation in the body; it also helps keep the body free of atherosclerosis. The same study done at Athens University showed that 4.3 million Britons who are over forty years of age suffer from erectile dysfunction. Over a couple of years, the Britons have tried to counter the condition with Viagra. Only a small percentage was successful with the drug, and those who did, the rectified condition did not last for long. When the same men tried the Mediterranean diet, over half of the percentage was successful, and those who failed did not follow the program to the latter.

However, the research does not completely spell out Viagra as a fail, no, the drug works, but at a very low rate compared to the Med diet. Worldwide, one out of two men who are between 40 and 70 years has an erectile dysfunction condition. Across the globe, Viagra is occasionally used to resolve the condition, but it comes with its grueling side effects. Though it assists in maintaining an erection, it causes back pain, headaches, and blurry vision.

According to Dr. Christina Chrysohoou, the sexual performance of middle-aged men and a few older men depended on physical exercises and a good diet. She said that those who practiced the Med Diet slashed the risk of the erectile condition by a whopping 40 percent. Also, she added that the diet could reduce the risk of acquiring metabolic syndrome that includes obesity, diabetes, and high blood pressure.

Chapter 4: How To Make The Mediterranean Diet Effective

Putting it together

Among the many, many diets, the Mediterranean diet is considered the best by most nutritionists. For those who first tried out on the diet, they attest that they will never switch to any other diet whatsoever. A few scientists say that when you start on the diet on the right note, you probably get assimilated and synchronized to it for a lifetime. Here are a few specific steps that will help you get started.

- **Eat your Fruits and Vegetables – and turn to whole grains**
  To a great extent, your meals should be made up of plant foods. Ensure that you get up to ten servings of fruits and veggies per day. Switch off pasta products and start taking a lot of whole grain rice. Whole grain bread and cereals will come in handy, too.

- **Go Nuts**
  While traveling or at work, keep a quick snack. Let the snack package comprise of walnuts, cashew nuts, almond, and pistachios. If you are an enthusiast of spreading bread, go for the natural peanut butter. It is the most preferred compared to those that contain hydrogenated fats. Probably, you have never tried Tahini which is sesame seeds that are blended; try it out as you start the med diet. Tahini serves as a dip as well.

- **For butter, pass it on**
  Instead of margarine and butter, use canola and olive oil, they are healthy alternatives. Use the oil while cooking or dip bread in spiced olive oil. You can spread the oil on bread (in our case, it should be whole

grained), it will serve as a splendid replacement to butter. Tahini will come in well for a spread or a dip.

- **Spice it up**
Salt in high amounts is harmful to your health, replace it with a selection of herbs as well as spices. They contain substances that are rich in nutrients that promote your health, and they will still make your food tasty and better. Reach out for natural spices and be lest assured that your meals would leave a lasting respite.

- **Go Fish**
Fish is worth the cost, so do as scientists insist, eat fish at least twice a week or more if you can. The best healthy choices are water-packed herring, trout, salmon, mackerel, and tuna. Grilled fish has a sense of good taste, though, but it requires a thorough clean up. If you have to go for fried fish, make sure it is sautéed using canola oil. Try to avoid fried fish as much as you can.

- **Skate with the red meat**
Okay, poultry may be your favorite dish, its mine too, but for the sake of the med diet, substitute for red meat. Choose the lean meat, and do not take big portions, but rather smaller amounts. Perhaps, you know a deck of playing cards, let the portion be equitable to it. Keep meats that are highly concentrated with fats at bay. They include sausage and bacon.

- **Select low-fat dairy**
You might have winced on this fact because you love ice cream and the finger-licking cheese. Avoid these dishes. If you have to go for them, eat low-fat cheese, skimmed milk, and yogurt that is free from fats. Two percent milk should be avoided as well as whole milk.

- **Raise a glass**

  If you love a slight tipple of wine from time to time, then cheers! Take wine as frequently as possible, especially during and after meals. If you dislike alcohol and have never started drinking, there's no need to start. There is an arsenal of alternatives, including the purple grape juice.

As you can see, the first major steps of the Mediterranean diet consist of typical foods which form a pattern of a healthy eating habit. The pattern is tried and true but is subject to alteration depending on bits of advice from your nutritionist.

How to improve on the Mediterranean diet

The ancient Mediterranean diet is considered a plant-based plan, but of course, not exclusively. Components like olive oil, and the most common one, wine, are typically fruit-based extracts. It means there are nutritional aspects of the diet that have been completely ignored. For instance, when wine interacts with metronidazole, it leads to headaches, vomiting, stomach upsets, sweating, and a racing heart. However, this wine can be professionally refined to curb such effects.

Another cogent example is the fact that the med diet includes a lot of white bread to a bigger percentage as compared to whole bread. You know that white bread is a result of processed white flour. During the process, white bread loses a significant amount of nutrients. As much as it loses nutrients, it may lead to accumulated weight of which the consequences are dire as discussed earlier. The remedy here is to scrap white bread as a component of the Mediterranean diet. If possible, cut it to 100% from the meal plan.

The other concept is that the diet encourages on consumption of cereals. On the contrary, consuming a lot of cereals means, in turn, that you take plenty of grains. As you well know, modern day grains are highly refined products — the traditional Mediterranean plan composed of unrefined cereals. There is nothing as difficult as a dieter going shopping and trying to isolate the refined grains and unprocessed ones. They end up picking the refined cereals as they are readily available and in high stocks in the market. What's the solution? Let's go back to the basics, insist on the traditional grains (whole grains) rather than using any available grains.

The diet is a plant-oriented diet, and following the diet to its finest details means taking a lot of veggies, beans, nuts, wine (has alcohol contents) fruits and other low-fat saturated food components. So, you would assume that your risk of getting cancer is entirely eliminated, it might be true, but not true to breast cancer. Alcohol is a widely known breast carcinogen, whether taken in moderation or not. So, the Mediterranean diet should be re-modified and alcohol eliminated from the diet's component. Such a move will assure you that the diet reduces the risk of breast cancer.

When you look at the modern-day Mediterranean diet, you will realize that it contains components that suggest sodium intake. You cannot ignore the fact that salt intake prompts diseases such as stroke, high blood pressure, and heart diseases. In fact, in America, salt intake is on the rise due to the fact that most Americans follow the modernized med diet. Most Americans take up to ten grams of salt per day through processed foods. Let's analyze the situation in a simple method. If we would reduce the intake by three grams, imagine the thousands of people, we would save .We could save thousands from stroke, a few thousand from heart attacks, and a dozen thousand from deaths.

Serving method

How do you serve your guests when they arrive at your house? Are they comfortable after a meal and say great things about your serving method? Well, don't fret about your serving style if it is not classy, because, towards the end of this book, you will be well-enlightened on proper serving methods.

When a guestcomes visiting, it is preferable to let them serve themselves in the kitchen rather than serving them. One of the most important reasonsfor this is because when you let them serve themselves, they are probably comfortable since not all of them eat the same amount of food. Another fact is that some of them may prefer certain foods to others. While others may serve themselves according to their doctor's prescription. It is probably for the best not only to let them serve themselves but also to make sure that the food you are preparing is well-balanced and won't favor some guests to others. It is more preferable to have a choice of more vegetables and lean protein.

Serving Wine

In most cases, people prefer taking wine while eating to having it after the meal. Well, in the Mediterranean diet, wine is inevitable and is highly recommended as part of the menu. Wine is preferred to be taken with meals because it improves the cholesterol levels in the body as well as helps in the digestion of food. As previously seen, it also reduces the chances of heart diseases by a big margin. Going by the medicinal implication of wine, white and red wine serve the same benefits to an individual. These two types of wine are not only best for special occasions but on all meals, especially lunch and dinner. It is a fact the Italians living in the Mediterranean region cannot go a day or even a meal without drinking wine.

Eating slowly

It might sound raving crazy, but food should be treatedin a special way, like a special person, the way you take care of that exceptional person. Such an approach will help you end up eating the food in the right way. Food should not be taken in a rush. Instead, take your time while still enjoying the sweet aroma in the air. Take small bites, apply the American table etiquette. Let your body relax, assume you have no other errands to attend to; your prime goal here is the boozy brunch.

The advantage of eating slowly is that you allow easy digestion of food. You also counter stomach upsets. Science has it that the human brain takes at least 15 minutes to sense that the stomach is full. The concept infers that if you eat faster, chances are that you will end up eating a lot, and by the time the brain communicates to you that your stomach is full, it will be passed the average time limit. The mishap may lead to discomforts through the day. Eating slowly also helps to ensure that you are not chocked. Chocking blocks the windpipe leading to breathing problems and the obvious worst scenario, death!

Dinner walks *good*

For you to attain a successful Mediterranean meal plan, it is wise to adhere to all the principles that come with the diet. Most people like to sit and lay down after dinner, which is totally not advisable. If you make a regular a habit of sitting idly after meals, a chance is that you are attracting lifestyle diseases such as chronic diabetes, obesity, heart diseases, andpsychological disorders. Med diet insists on a walk after a meal. It is more advisable to do a nature walk or engage in physical activities. It is well believedthat the Mediterranean diet prompts to bring people together and some even end up in marriages through interactions brought about by nature walks. Practically, the belief may be true. You realize that the diet does not only make you a healthy individual but also improves your social part of life. Coincidentally, you may not be a dinner walk connoisseur, but you can go for healthy activities after a meal. Music works perfectly well since it triggers you to dance. A dance combined with a little tipple of wine makes a great blend.

Chapter 5: Diseases the Mediterranean Diet Prevents

It is true to say that most diets, in fact, all of them, target on curing and preventing diseases. Researchers put it that, among the numerous numbers of diets available across the globe, the Mediterranean diet has the largest number of diseases it caters for. PREDIMED, which means prevention with the Mediterranean diet, is the largest group to ever carry out a study on the med diet. It revealed that the diet's components, especially, olive oil, nuts ,and almonds, reduces the chances of being diagnosed with cardiovascular diseases by a bigger margin, 30% to be precise.

Below is a list of some of the diseases that the Mediterranean diet prevents and helps treat.

- Heart diseases
- Chronic diseases
- Circulatory diseases
- Blindness diseases
- Allergies
- Asthma ✓
- Cancer
- Depression
- Diabetes
- Metabolic syndrome

Heart disease

The heart is one of the most crucial and sensitive parts of the body. The heart performs a lot of critical functions in the body; it is right to say that it performs 80% of the entire body's functions. It does so through pumping and circulating blood in the body. Now that you are enlightened on this fact, I suppose you dread on ever contracting any of the heart diseases. For most people, they would prefer having an alert bell that signals when the diseases try to creep in their body. That is just a mere fantasy. The reality in preventing these deadly diseases is following the Mediterranean diet to its finest details. The fact that the diet is rich in healthy nutrients drawn from fruits, vegetables, legumes, and whole grains, makes the diet the ultimate remedy for the diseases.

Common types of heart diseases include:

- Cardiac arrest
- High blood pressure
- Coronary artery disease

Sign and symptom of heart diseases

a) Chest pain
Chest pain is mostly caused by the coronary artery. Chest pain is known to bring a lot of discomforts in the body especially when you are coughing. Chest pain may switch to other areas such as the neck if the coughing continues for long.

b) Profuse sweating
You will wake up late in the night and find your bed wet, especially on your head section. This means you have been sweating all night long. Other people sweat all over the body making it very difficult to enjoy a nap.

c) Weak body
Maybe you are used to handling your house chores in a jiffy, but this time around, you find yourself unusually weak. You are not even able to attend to

easy tasks or even run a simple errand, that's a sign of heart disease.

d) Increased heartbeat rate
When you are suffering from any heart diseases, the body seems to spot danger. Naturally, the only way to cope with the situation is for the body to increase its heartbeat rate in an effort to supply enough blood and oxygen.

e) Fainting
The heart takes care of the rest of the body, and when it experiences just a little mishap, it triggers the body to break down. Scientifically, the break down is called fainting. Fainting is common when you have symptoms of arrhythmia disease. Also, if you are just about to experience heart failure, you have a lot of fainting episodes.

Chronic Diseases

Did you know that some diseases are based on the age and sex of an individual? Well, now you know. According to researches, most of the chronic diseases affect mostly the old people in the community and women when it comes to gender.Going by the CDC reports, chronic diseases are top in the list in killing adults who are 65 years and above. In 2014 alone, the diseases killed 489,722 people.A forum known as Federal Interagency showed that 26% of women who were pregnant and those who were breastfeeding were killed by the diseases.

Sign and symptoms of chronic diseases

a) Memory loss

Memory loss is a very common symptom of chronic diseases. If you occasionally find yourself forgetting people and things, then you are all set for a chronic disease. Don't fret and get scared of this fact, there are remedies for the memory loss condition. Avoid prescription medicine, they are known to do more harm other than solving the situation. Sleep adequately and get rid of poisonous substances in your house. Eat organic foods only, especially Paleo foods. Use spices on meals instead of sodium. It is also prudent to seek professional home therapy.

b) Sore throats

Sore throats will make you lose appetite for food. There is that painful wince that cuts across your throat every time you intend to swallow food. Due to this discomfort, you will give up on eating food. Sometimes, you will sense no taste in food, especially foods with a sweet sensation. Sore throats tend to destroy the tasting sensory organ.

c) Fatigue

This is when you wake up in the morning and still want to go back to bed. Your body becomes wearingly weak, despite the fact that you have not performed any upheaval tasks. You find it hard lifting things, and you also start feeling pain in the joints, muscles tweak in pain, and they turn pale red.

d) Headaches

As it happens to almost everyone, whether you are a menial worker or you work in an office setting, experiencing headaches is inevitable. However, when the headache is prolonged, it might be a sign of chronic disease. Headache is a medical disorder that depicts high blood pressure.

Circulatory Diseases

They are also called cardiovascular diseases.They include:

- Atherosclerosis
- Heart attack
- Mitral valve prolapse
- Mitral valve regurgitation
- Mitral stenosis
- Angina pectoris
- Dysrhythmia
- Arrhythmia
- Heart failure
- High cholesterol
- Hypertension
- Cardiac Ischemia
- Stroke
- Aortic aneurysms
- Peripheral artery disease
- Venous thromboembolism

Blindness Disease

The truth is that nobody would ever want to be blind, even for one second. You can imagine all that pressure of not being able to see someone or something for your entire life. Blindness affects the mental status of an individual. They are used to seeing things, and now, they are faced with the bitter truth that they'll never see again. Their self-esteem drops to zero, some even lose hope in life and end up committing suicide. The virgin olive oil and nuts are very important in a diet as they help in reducing the chances of blindness to almost nil.

Signs and symptoms

Blindness is caused by many factors including cataract, head injury, diabetes among others. Blindness can be temporary or permanent depending on the cause and how deep the cause has on the head.

- Flushes on the eye
- Hazy eyes
- Double vision
- Pain in the eyes

Allergies

Thisis the irritating result that occurs when the body reacts to the environment or certain foods. You may end up disliking the foods even for a lifetime. Allergies are detrimental because they come with a lot of restrictions on good foods. In most cases, the doctor would go ahead and write new prescriptions of foods that you are expected to eat and offer helpful advice on the same foods. The Mediterranean diet is based on traditional organic foods and seldom do they have side effects that may cause allergies.

Sign and symptoms

a) Sneezing
   Sneezing is the most common symptom when it comes to allergy. This can be because of some foods or even the common one, dust.

b) Itchiness
   Itchiness is another irritating sensation. You find yourself scratching a particular part of your body and sometimes all over your body. Itching leads to hives or rashes.

c) Red eyes
   Allergy also causes red and fatigued eyes. Redness of the eyes may lead to conjunctivitis. Prolonged red eyes can signal glaucoma.

Asthma Attacks

This is a condition in which the body produces extra mucus that often blocks the windpipes and causes breathing problems. Doctors introduced plastic asthma to help breathers which are readily available in the health units. The Mediterranean diet has been proven to prevent these attacks. The diet ensures that the body is fed with appropriate foods that have the right nutrients.

Sign and symptoms

There are three main signs of Asthma attacks:

- Trouble with sleep
  Statistically, in the usual eight hours of sleep, you will only sleep for three hours. You will experience severe and continuous coughing. Incidentally, you develop chest pains and have watery eyes; all these are signs of an asthma attack.

- Short on breath
  You will experience multiple bouts of cut breathe, especially at night. Of course, you will struggle with sleeping, sound sleep will be far-fetched.

- Fast heartbeat
  The heart will beat twice the rate it is usedto. You will find it hard to breathe and occasionally gasp for air. It becomes difficult for you to take a short walk or a light jog. Your exercise life will be slowed down since you'll tire up quickly.

Cancer

There are very many forms of cancer, and almost all of them are deadly. Chances of surviving cancers are very minimal. This is because, cancer, unlike many other diseases exposes its symptoms when it is too late. Research doctors re-affirm that the hopes of surviving cancer are very slim or next to none. The following is a list of some common types of cancers.

- Lung cancer
- Bladder cancer
- Prostate cancer
- Breast cancer
- Melanoma

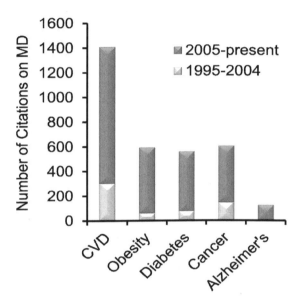

It is reported that breast cancer is among the leading cause of death for most women in the United States. They say breast cancer comes without warning. The Mediterranean diet is very important because it helps in killing cancer bacteria that are located in women's breasts.

The Mediterranean diet prevents these types of cancer through its wide range of foods that provide nutrients that are essential in curbing cancer bacteria. It offers natural organic food components rather than refined foods that are associated with causing cancer.

Sign and symptom

a) Loss of Appetite

Also known as decreased appetite, medically the situation is referred to as anorexia. When the loss of appetite is prolonged, you lose weight and probably suffer from malnutrition.

b) Fever

A fever is a response to an infection. Your body temperature is higher than normal. You are considered to have a fever when your body temperature goes beyond 37 degrees Celsius. Symptoms of fever include lethargy, feeling cold, and shivering.

c) Blood in urine

When you go to the toilet for a short call, you will see blood coming out while you are urinating. Blood in urine is caused by a lot of factors, it might be due to bruises caused by rough sex (rape). Cancer is one of them especially if the condition is continuous.

d) Prolonged cough

Coughing once or twice is very normal. It might be due to a cold environment. However, if you experience a continuous cough, it is a cause of alarm. It is sensible to seek a professional check-up.

e) Having trouble with swallowing

Having trouble in swallowing is also referred to as dysphagia. It is a sign your esophagus has a problem. Acute dysphagia may be a sign of throat cancer.

f) Swelling of the prostate gland

The prostate gland is the one that emits the fluid that contains sperms. It is located around the urethra. An enlarged prostate gland may be a sign of prostate cancer.

Depression

Most people are oblivious of the fact that depression is a disease. They assume that it is just an uncontrolled state of mind. It might be true, but medically,depression is classified just like any other form of a disease. It is also defined as a mood disorder. It is an extreme feeling of anger, sadness, and loss. The impacts of depression are very dire; they lead to isolation, low self-esteem, and the worst of all, suicide.

Signs and symptoms of depression

a) Mood swings
Once or twice a week, most Americans undergo bouts of mood swings. They are also called mood disorders. It simply means that you occasionally experience episodes of extreme happiness or extreme sadness.

b) Abnormal Behavior
A depressed person may do things to the extreme. They indulge in excessive alcohol drinking. A depressed person may suddenly turn to a workaholic. They switch to hysterical behaviors like laughing extensively or crying non- stop.

c) Weight loss or gain

This is the most common scenario that always happens to most people. Losing weight is most common than gaining weight unless eating is what cools your nerves down. A depressed person will end up skinny very fast because of refusing to eat; they have noappetite for food anymore.

d) Excessive sleep
Depression is known to cause excessive sleep as a method of isolation. A depressed person will sleep at odd hours to avoid meeting with people.

Diabetes

In the US, diabetes is considered among the deadliest diseases. Healthy meals are encouraged, and especially the Mediterranean diet is emphasized. This is a condition that normally comes based on too much sugar consumption and obviously leading to high sugar levels in the blood. The Mediterranean diet ensures that the sugar levels are keptincheck.

Sign and symptoms

a) Dry mouth
In medical terms, dry mouth is also called xerostomia. Diabetes causes dry mouth due to an increased level of glucose. Xylimelts product cures dry mouth.

b) A lot of hunger
When diabetes goes uncontrolled, it is called hyperglycemia. Due to low levels of insulin, glucose cannot enter the body cells. As a result, the food that you take is hardly converted into energy; hunger creeps in.

Metabolic syndrome

Metabolic syndrome is also referred to as syndrome X, other doctors called it dysmetabolic syndrome. The main elements of syndrome X are abnormal cholesterol, insulin resistance, resistance to clotting, and hypertension. Some other factors associated with the condition include accumulated fat around the waist of an individual, breathing problems, dizziness, high blood pressure, and increasedbloodsugar. Nutritionists advocate for the engagement of the Mediterranean diet for the effective curbing of the disease.

It is now evident that most of these diseases are associated with high levels of fats in the body. Fats increase the level of LDL cholesterol, and in return, it reduces the level of the beneficial HDL cholesterol.

Definition of Fat

Fat is a mixture of carbon and hydrogen atoms that are rich in energy. The energy generated is the best when it comes to building muscles during exercises.

What makes people fat?

Here is what you didn't know, fat does not make you fat, but calories do. If you eat a lot of food rich in calories, the level of calories in your body will increase,and the level of your body mass will also increase making you big up to an obese size. The more you consume, the bigger you grow.

Facts about fat

- It goes well with protein as the two work hand-in-hand
- Fat helps to boost your body functioning.

- Fat is found in all types of food even water
- The right consumption of fat does not make you fat
- Fat has a lot of benefits attached to it

Benefits of fat

1. Rich in vitamins
   Eating vegetables without any fat is useless; a proper lunch of vegetables should not miss out on fat even if it is a small amount of it. Fat is rich in vitamin A, D, E and K.

   Vitamin A- This vitamin is very important when it comes to growth and development, it helps the body to grow stronger and stronger each day as the right nutrients are added to it.

   Vitamin D- Vitamin D is important when it comes to the structuring of the bones. This vitaminmakes sure that your bones grow out to be strong as they are well-developed.

   Vitamin E- Immunity is everything. Body immunity is what keeps your body away from many diseases. Vitamin E is important in building your immunity.

   Vitamin K- When you are involved in an injury, and you realize that your body is not healing fast, then you should know that you are not eating enough fats. Vitamin K is there to make sure that your blood clotting works fast and you don't bleed too much.

2. Maintain cell membrane health
   Fat is responsible for developing hormones in your body. When you have enough fat in your body, your skin becomes very smooth as the hormones are very active in the body. Those people with rough skins and hard hair

are lacking out on fat, and they should consider ensuring that their food has enough fat.

3. Gives the body energy
As stated earlier, fat and protein work well to give your body energy. This energy can sustain you for long, even if you overstay in your outdoor activities. It means that the fats will be converted into energy.

4. Hormonal production
Fats play a very vital role in the production of hormones. These hormones are responsible for the changes that happen in the human body. The changes include the puberty stage, adolescent stage, and menopause. They are also helpful in fighting both external and internal diseases, this is through the involvement of the white blood cells.

Types of Fats

There are three major types of fats: the polyunsaturated, monounsaturated, and lastly, the saturated fat.

1. Saturated Fats
Saturated fat is commonly based on animals and plants. Some of the plant products that contain these fats include the coconut plant, whose oil is used for cooking. Animal products that contain fats include eggs, milk, and meat. It is true that saturated fats cause heart diseases and so they should be avoided at all costs.

2. Monounsaturated
Monounsaturated fat comes from the words saturated fat. This might not be as common as the saturated fat, but it is the one that is used when it comes to dieting. The monounsaturated fats comprise of extra virgin olive oil, cashew nuts,

walnuts, and avocado. Olive oil is the best when not processed. It is commonly preferred when it comes to maintaining proper body size, especially when served with lemon juice or natural yogurt.

3. Polyunsaturated
   This is the third category of fats; in this category, we have the popular omega 3 and 6. Omega 3 is found in flaxseed and fish. The three components of omega 3 are Alpha-linolenic acid, docosahexaenoic acid, and eicosatetraenoic acid. Omega 6 fats are found in borage and primrose oil. The common component of omega 6 fats is linolenic acid.

Chapter 6: Rules to Lose Weight

The Mediterranean diet offers an arsenal of ways of losing weight. As a beginner, you can adopt one or several of the following ways of losing weight. They are plain simple and painless too.

- **Don't miss breakfast**
  You may assume that skipping your breakfast will help you shed off those extra pounds. That is a huge misconception. The truth is, at the end of the day, you will have eaten more than you expected. Research has it that those who take breakfast acquire a lower BMI than those who skip. In fact, they perform better at school and in the office. Take whole grain cereal, a bowl if you wish, plus a fruit.

- **At night, forget about the kitchen**
  Don't creep into the kitchen at night for mindless munches, in fact, scientist advice that you brush your teeth to avoid any more eating through the night. If you must eat, suck on hard candy, or light ice cream or perhaps frozen yogurt.

- **Be wise on liquid calories**
  Of course, you know that sweet drinks capitalize on calories but rarely satisfy your hunger. Quench your thirst with water, especially citrus water. Try fruit juice, but should be 100% fruit juice. Take milk that is low-fat or skimmed.

- **Eat more produce**
  The fruits and vegetables you eat should be low in calorie. Instead of piling your plate with a full brunch of meat, slide the meat off and pile more vegetables. For

dinner or lunch, you can start with broth soup or a vegetable salad.

- **Prefer the Grain**
Instead of taking refined grains such as cookies, white bread, pretzels, and cakes, eat whole grains. They contain fiber that makes you fill up quickly which implies that you will only eat a sensible portion.

- **Control Your Environments**
Check on what you are stocking the kitchen with, ensure that the foods are healthy ones rather than junk foods. Avoid restaurants that sell all types of foods, 'all you want restaurants.'

- **Trim Portions**
If you reduce your food portions by 10 to 20%, you would definitely trim that weight. You realize that the portions served, whether at home or in the restaurant, are beyond what you need. It is wise to get a portion control gadget, probably a small plate or a cup.

- **Add more steps**
A pedometer will work here, work on the steps, and let the target be at least 10,000 per day. Take the dog for a walk, get more active throughout the day. The pedometer serves as a reminder and a constant motivator.

- **Have a snack at every meal**
A healthy snack ensures that you are constantly full and you will not overindulge in eating. Your sugar levels are kept steady as well.

- **Turn to lighter alternatives**
While doing salad dressing, make sure you use products that are low in fats. Switch to salsa to act as a dip; hummus can work, too.

Why lose weight?

- Less joint pain
- You will eliminate the stigma
- Your new look may get you a new job
- You will eradicate depression
- Your sex life will improve
- You will improve your memory
- Your skin complexion will brighten up
- Your confidence will heighten
- Your mood will definitely improve
- You will stop snoring
- You will be able to try new activities

Rules to Losing Weight

- Eat a lot of fiber foods.
- Ensure that you measure your weight often for motivation.
- Make sure you exercise a lot.
- Be sugar-free, avoid them at all cost especially ice cream and creamy yogurt.
- Make sure you eat a lot of protein in the morning.
- Make sure to have a good night sleep of at least 8 hours a day.
- Focus on good things and avoid being stressed.

Exercises for losing weight

There are a few regular yet simple and comfortable forms of exercises you can indulge in for effective weight loss.

1. Running
   Are you running and not losing weight? The answer might be probably yes, adjust your running calendar. A

thirty-minute run or a twenty-minute run per week would definitely not burn those unwanted calories. Losing one pound per week requires you to slash five hundred calories per day. Of course, you will combine the running with a good diet.

2. Hikes
   Hiking was started out as a recreation activity and was done as a hobby during free time. Today, hiking is not only a hobby but also a medical plan. According to various researches, hiking has a great impact on weight loss and health maintenance. It helps in reducing problems associated with heart diseases. Improves the blood pressure level, hiking is also known to improve body balance and boost the body muscles.

3. Swimming
   Swimming is not only a great sport but an exercise as well. It is an effective healthy exercise since it involves exercising every part of the body. It ensures that muscles are built stronger and helps the heart attain a healthy pumping rate. Your mind gets rejuvenated, and your body tuned-up.

4. Lunges
   The forward lunge is effective for losing weight. It works on a variety of muscles simultaneously. Involve the quads, hamstrings, and the glutes for a big burn on the calories. Stand straight and tall while holding your hips, step forward with either your left or right foot. Your spine should remain tall, drop your body slowly until you form a ninety-degree body shape, pause and bring your leg home for another start. Repeat the exercise for at least ten times on both sides; perform three sets of the exercise.

5. Cross Fit

Cross fit has grown to be a very popular form of exercise in recent times, but do not overindulge in it. It is important to select the box (cross-fit) which will fit perfectly on you. If you are not sure about the cross fit, seek help from a certified coach. The coach should be able to modify the moves that will match well with you.

Basics Before the Lifting Weights

- Squats
Squats work on quads, hips, hamstrings, and glutes. The resultant effect of squats is a good body density, body balance, and coordination

- Pull-ups and push-ups
For a pull, make sure you involve the forearms, the lats, biceps, core, and your mid back. For the push-ups, engage shoulders, triceps, core, and chest. In between the two exercises, you realize that your whole body is fully engaged.

- Treadmill
Walking on the treadmill is an aerobic exercise. The exercise burns calories significantly. When combined with a good diet such as the Mediterranean diet, it works perfectly well. The treadmill is preferable for the beginners who are not ready for outdoor running or walking.

Tips for Beginners in the Gym

- Let fitness be a habit
- Control your lifts
- Employ compounds movements
- Ensure perfect posture
- Follow a diet

- Squeeze the lifts, but not for more than two seconds
- Learn from your failures
- Finish the routine
- Ask questions
- Concentrate on your muscles

Chapter 7: 7-Day Meal Plan

The Mediterranean Diet is one of the healthiest diets of all times. The concept behind the notion is that, with the diet, you eat just like the people living within the Mediterranean region. Your meals consist of vegetables, healthy fats, nuts, fish, legumes, whole grains, and regulated amounts of wine.

This seven-day meal plan consists of delicious, nutritious meals. It is a week of having very healthy meals. It is a 1,500-calorie meal which is a journey of losing one to two pounds per week.   Take   a   look!

Helpful Tips While Preparing the Seven Day Meal Plan

- On day one, while preparing dinner, it is wise to prepare the Basic Quinoa in a batch. You will use the leftovers on day six (lunch), day three (dinner), and day two (lunch).
- Prepare the Roasted Root Vegetables on the sheet pan; the leftovers will be used for lunch on the sixth and fourth days and the second day as well. You will also use them on day five for dinner.
- Make the Herb Vinaigrette that will be enough for the whole week.

Benefits of Planning Meals

- Less Stress
  The perk of sticking a meal plan on the door of your fridge is that you will have a well-organized mind of what you will be cooking throughout the week. You will not have to make the last minute dash looking for what to cook.

- Save Money

  Now that you have penned down the meal plan, it is essential to write a shopping list as well. The list will be based on the plan. The list will ward you off from impulse buying. You will only buy what you need. Critics put it that, people save a significant amount of money when they shop once, as compared to when they have multiple shopping sprees within a given time frame, say a week.

- Eat Healthy Foods

  Since you will not rush to the food outlets in the last minute, you will avoid eating frozen foods that are normally stocked in these food joints. A meal plan allows you to put quality time while organizing it. Hence all the healthy ingredients are put in place as well. As a result, your family will have healthy meals duly prepared.

  Healthy eating entails eating fresh food, and as you know, fresh food has a very short shelf-life; a meal plan will come in handy to help you achieve this goal of eating fresh food.

- A Meal Plan gives you Control

  A meal plan keeps your eating habits in check, it depicts the initial steps towards achieving a healthy life. The plan acts as an outline of what and when to eat. The beneficial ingredients are all set for you already, rather than when you would just go out and eat anything that comes your way. You are able to attend to other important matters of life with confidence since you know that your food is already sorted.

- Creates Food Awareness

  During the process of preparing the meal plan, and since the ingredients are professionally developed, you learn a lot about food. You will get enlightened on what food does what to your body. Also, you are accountable to your own health and that of your household; you get to know the merits and demerits of the wide range of foods.

- Save Time
  When you do not have a meal plan, you spent a lot of time wandering around the market aimlessly; you have no specific foods you intend to buy. When a meal plan is in place, you are sure of what to buy.

- Controls Food Wastage
  In the year 2011, the average amount of food that was wasted in every Canadian house amounted to $1,120. The meal plan will definitely help you manage your food purchases in a better way. Failing to have a meal plan is like draining money down the dust bin. Food wastage is brought by forgetting the foods that still lie in the fridge. An updated inventory of the pantry as well as the fridge while preparing the meal plan ensures that the food rotation is intact, thereby, curbing food wastage, and most importantly, money.

Okay, you may say that you have a busy life, we all do. We have hectic routines ,and sometimes, mealtimes or cooking pose as a very humongous task. The benefits of having a meal plan outweigh those of totally ignoring it. So, why not get a cut and enjoy the benefits of preparing a meal plan, the perks outweigh the drawbacks, and it won't cost a dime!

Day 1

Fig, Balsamic, And Ricotta Toast

Preparation time-> 20 minutes

Cooking time-> 15 minutes

Ingredients:

- 6 slice of dough bread
- Olive oil, preferably extra virgin
- ½ tablespoon for honey
- Balsamic vinegar
- 6 figs
- Tomato juice

Cooking method

1. Heat a pan over medium heat. Sear the bread on both sides with olive oil, put in the pan to cook for 4 minutes while flipping the sides.
2. While doing that,prepare the ricotta and put it in a bowl with pepper and honey.
3. Put aside the cooked toast and sprinkle or smear it with the ricotta mixture.
4. Serve with tomato juice when done and enjoy.

----*Midmorning snack*----

Plums

Preparation time -> 5 minutes

Preparation method

1. Access 3 plums cut into four sides
2. Serve and enjoy.

----*Lunch*----

Mediterranean Salad

Preparation time-> 15 minutes

Cooking time-> 15 minutes

Ingredients:

- Salad green mix 3 cups
- 1 cup of cucumber (sliced)
- 2tablespoon of olive oil
- 3tablespoon of carrot (grated)
- Balsamic vinegar 2 cups
- 8 dough bread slices pita
- Pepper
- ½ hummus

Cooking method

1. Put all ingredients together: cucumber, carrot, and greens in a bowl.
2. Pour vinegar and oil in the bowl, sprinkle with pepper and salt.
3. Serve with hummus, pita and enjoy!

----*Afternoon snack*----

Raspberry

***Preparation time*->** 5 minutes

1. 2 cups of raspberry

----***Dinner***----

Chicken Chili with Sweet Potatoes

***Preparation time*->**10 minutes

***Cooking time*->**40 minutes

Ingredients:

- Chicken chili with sweet potatoes coupled
- ¼ diced avocado and 1 tablespoon of non-fat plain yogurt.

<u>Cooking instructions</u>

1. Heat oil then add the ingredients that are available.
2. Add the chicken pieces to it then fry it for 4 minutes.
3. Heat vegetable oil then add spring onions and fry.
4. Add the ingredients and stir.
5. Add the fried chicken pieces and stir well. Serve warm with some noodles and yogurt

Day 2

Raspberry with Muesli

Preparation time-> 20 minutes

Cooking time-> 15 minutes

Ingredients:

- 4 cups apple juice
- 4 cups rolled oats
- 3 green apples (grated)
- 3 tablespoon vanilla
- 500g raspberry
- 3 tablespoon honey
- 3 cups of yogurt (natural)
- 3 tablespoon vanilla essence

Cooking method

1. Open fire and heat the juice in the pan for at least 3 minutes until warm.

2. Assemble vanilla and oats to a big bowl and pour your warm juice there.
3. Place in a freezer for 30 minutes until the juiced is soaked.
4. Remove it from the freezer, add raspberries and apple on the top and mix.
5. Add the natural yogurt, honey, and vanilla and stir them well.
6. Place the oat mixture in a glass and serve.
7. Enjoy.

----Lunch----

Roasted Quinoa Salad

Preparation time-> 10 minutes

Cooking time-> 25 minutes

Ingredients:

- 1 red onion
- 1 cup sweet potato
- 1 cup zucchini
- 2 cup tomato (cherry)
- 1 lemon
- 5 tablespoons olive oil
- Salt, pepper
- 1 cup fresh parsley
- 2 tablespoon apple
- 5 cup quinoa

Cooking method

1. Heat the oven till warm.
2. Add ingredients: onion, corn, tomatoes, sweet potatoes, and zucchini to the baking sheet in the oven.
3. Make juice with the lemon.

4. Pour olive oil to the lemon juice and then add salt and pepper.
5. Roast the veggie for 25 minutes.
6. Add quinoa to the transferred bowl of roasted veggie and toss them well.
7. Mix apple cider with olive oil in another bowl and make sure to toss them, too.
8. Lastly, access the parsley and garnish, serve and enjoy.

----*Afternoon snack*----

10 peanuts will be enough to keep you going until dinner time.

----*Dinner*----

Carrot and Chickpea Salad

Preparation time-> 5 minutes

Cooking time-> 25 minutes

Ingredients:

- Clove garlic
- ½ cup olive oil
- Lemon
- 2 (15 1/2 –ounce) cans chickpeas rinsed and drained
- Ground cumin ½
- 3 carrots
- ½ teaspoon salt

Cooking method

1. Make juice from the lemon.
2. Combine all the ingredients together: lemon juice, salt, olive oil, and chickpeas and place them in a blender.

3. Stir them a bit, transfer to a bowl, and place them on a freezer for 2 hours.
4. Cut and peel the carrots.
5. Serve with hummus and enjoy.

Day 3

Fig and Ricotta Toast

Preparation time-> 5 minutes

Cooking time-> 10 minutes

Ingredients:

- 2 fig (sliced)
- 2 teaspoon sesame
- 2 dash cinnamon
- 2 teaspoon honey
- ½ cup skim ricotta
- 3 slice whole wheat

Cooking method

1. Pick a bowl, combine skim ricotta with cinnamon and honey.
2. Smear the combination on whole wheat toast.
3. Spread some sesame seeds and fig.
4. Serve with tomato juice and enjoy.

----*Mid-morning snack*----

Preparation time ->5 minutes

2 plums

----*Lunch*----

Tomato & Artichoke Gnocchi

Preparation time->10 minutes

Cooking time->20 minutes

Ingredients:

- 1 tablespoon salt and garlic
- 3 Olive oil
- Tomatoes
- 1 jar Artichoke hearts (chopped)
- 2 tablespoon Basil fresh
- 6 ounces of cheese
- 2 tablespoon oregano
- Gnocchi 1 package

Cooking instructions

1. Heat olive oil in a pan.
2. Add salt and sauté until golden.
3. Add ingredients: artichokes, tomatoes, basil, and oregano.
4. Boil for 7 minutes.
5. Put half-size water in a pan heat, then add gnocchi and boil until you start seeing it float up to the water.
6. Stir all of them until they fully blend for about 7 minutes.
7. Serve while hot and enjoy.

----Afternoon snack----

Raspberry and Greek yogurt

Preparation time->5 minutes

Ingredients:

- 2 tablespoon almonds (sliced)
- 2 cup raspberry
- ½ cup of Greek yogurt

Preparation method

1. Pick raspberry, mix Greek yogurt and almonds, then top with a raspberry.
2. Serve and enjoy.

----Dinner----

Fish Fillet

Preparation time->10 minutes

Cooking time->40 minutes

Ingredients:

- Onion (chopped)
- Olive oil
- Tomatoes
- ½ cup white wine
- Chopped parsley 2 tablespoon
- Sugar preferably 1 teaspoon
- Salt and pepper ¼ teaspoon
- Fish fillet 1 kg
- Cream 2 cups

Cooking instructions

1. Heat the oven and fry chopped and peeled onion until golden brown.
2. Add tomatoes and stir them all together for 1 minute.
3. Add other ingredients: parsley, sugar, salt, pepper, and wine.
4. Continue stirring while boiling then add the fish fillet and continue stirring while flipping on each side.
5. Cook for 8 minutes.
6. Set aside. Pick cream and stir well in medium heat while tasting.
7. Pour your fish fillet when the cream is tasty and cook for another 2 minutes.
8. Serve with brown rice and side salad while hot and enjoy.

Day 4

Creamy Blueberry and Pecan Oats

Cooking time-> 10 minutes

Ingredients:

- Salt, ¼ tablespoon
- Water, 1 cup
- 1 cup Rolled oats
- 1 cup blueberry
- 3 maple tablespoons
- 3tablespoons of Greek yogurt
- Toasted pecans preferably 2teaspoons

Cooking method

1. Heat the pan.
2. Boil half full of water. Add salt.
3. Add oats and stir oats then cook for 5 minutes.
4. Ensure that water is completely absorbed while stirring.
5. Remove after 5 minutes and give it time to cool.

6. Add pecan, blueberries, and yogurt.
7. Serve and enjoy.

----*Midmorning snack*----

Orange

Preparation time-> 3 minutes

Preparation method

Cut into pieces after peeling the skin off and enjoy.

----*Lunch*----
Roasted Quinoa Salad

Preparation time-> 10 minutes

Cooking time-> 25 minutes

Ingredients:

- 1 red onion
- 1 cup sweet potato
- 1 cup zucchini
- 2 cup tomato (cherry)
- 1 lemon
- 5 tablespoons olive oil
- Salt, pepper
- 1 cup fresh parsley

- 2 tablespoon apple
- 5 cup quinoa

Cooking method

1. Heat the oven till warm.
2. Add ingredients: onion, corn, tomatoes, sweet potatoes, and zucchini to the baking sheet in the oven.
3. Make juice with the lemon.
4. Pour olive oil to the lemon juice and then add salt and pepper.
5. Roast the veggie for 25 minutes.
6. Add quinoa to the transferred bowl of roasted veggie and toss them well.
7. Mix apple cider with olive oil in another bowl and make sure to toss them, too.
8. Lastly, access the parsley and garnish, serve and enjoy.

----*Dinner*----

Chicken and White Beans

Preparation time->30 minutes

Cooking time->1 hour

Ingredients:

- ½tablespoon vegetable oil
- 3 chicken breasts
- White beans
- 3 cups chicken broth
- Pepper and salt teaspoon
- Peeled and chopped onions
- ¾ cup of water
- Ground cumin

Cooking instructions

1. Heat oven with less heat.
2. Place broth and beans and cover them. Cover for two hours.
3. In another cooker, pour olive oil and boil for 20 seconds then add chicken and salt.
4. After a minute, add pepper. Flip the chicken on sides while cooking for 6 minutes.
5. Drain after the minutes are over.
6. Continue cooking by adding ingredients: chilies, onion mixture, and garlic.
7. Add water when done and let it cook.
8. Cook for 30 minutes while stirring.
9. Remove beans from the other cooker and set in a plate then add chicken.
10. Serve while hot and enjoy.

Day 5

Raspberry with Muesli

Preparation time-> 20 minutes

Cooking time-> 15 minutes

Ingredients:

- 4 cups apple juice
- 4 cups rolled oats
- 3 green apples (grated)
- 3 tablespoon vanilla
- 500g raspberry
- 3 tablespoon honey
- 3 cups of yogurt (natural)
- 3 tablespoon vanilla essence

Cooking method

1. Open fire and heat the juice in the pan for at least 3 minutes until warm.
2. Assemble vanilla and oats to a big bowl and pour your warm juice there.
3. Place in a freezer for 30 minutes until the juiced is soaked.
4. Remove it from thefreezer. Add raspberries and apple on the top and mix.
5. Add the natural yogurt, honey, and vanilla and stir them well.
6. Place the oat mixture in a glass and serve.
7. Enjoy.

----*Midmorning snack*----

Cucumber and Vinaigrette

Preparation time-> 5 minutes

Preparation method

1. Mix cucumber and vinaigrette together.
2. Serve and enjoy.

----**Lunch**----

Tomato & Artichoke Gnocchi

Preparation time ->10 minutes

Cooking time->20 minutes

Ingredients:

- 1 tablespoon Salt garlic
- 3 Olive oil
- Tomatoes
- 1 jar Artichoke hearts (chopped)
- 2 tablespoon Basil fresh
- 6 ounces of cheese
- 2 tablespoon oregano
- Gnocchi 1 package

Cooking instructions

1. Heat olive oil in a pan.
2. Add salt and sauté until golden.
3. Add ingredients: artichokes, tomatoes, basil, and oregano

4. Boil for 7 minutes.
5. Put half-size water in a pan and heat, then add gnocchi and boil until you start seeing it float up in the water.
6. Stir all of them until they fully blend for about 7 minutes.
7. Serve while hot and enjoy.

----*Afternoon snack*----

Orange

Preparation time-> 3 minutes

Preparation method

Cut into pieces after peeling the skin off and enjoy.

----*Dinner*----

Roasted Root Vegetables With Goat Cheese

Preparation time->10 minutes

Cooking time->50 minutes

Ingredients:

- Fresh thyme
- 3 peppers green
- 2 two onions
- Salt
- Olive oil
- Goat cheese ¼ kg
- Parsley

Cooking instructions

1. Heat the oven.

2. Add olive oil to the pan.
3. Add the ingredients: onion, pepper.
4. Add salt and thyme.
5. Add vegetables and roast for 20 minutes.
6. Serve with cheese and parsley and enjoy

Day 6

Creamy Blueberry And Pecan Oats

Preparation time-> 5 minutes

Cooking time-> 10 minutes

Ingredients:

- Salt, ¼ tablespoon
- Water, 1 cup
- 1 cup Rolled oats
- 1 cup blueberry
- 3 maple tablespoon
- 3 tablespoon of Greek yogurt
- Toasted pecans preferably 2 teaspoon

Cooking method

1. Heat the pan.
2. Boil half full of water. Add salt.
3. Add oats and stir the oats then cook for 5 minutes.
4. Ensure that water is completely absorbed while stirring.
5. Remove after 5 minutes and give it time to cool.
6. Add pecan, blueberries, and yogurt.
7. Serve and enjoy.

----*Lunch*----

Chickpea and Veggie Grain

Cooking time->10 minutes

Ingredients:

- Lemmon juice
- Garlic salt
- Parsley
- 3 Ounces cauliflower
- Tamari

- Chicken peas ½ sumac teaspoon
- ½ cup Brown rice
- Tahini paste ½ tablespoon
- Greek yogurt

Cooking instructions

1. Boil water.
2. Slice and peel the ingredients and add them.
3. Boil for 10 minutes.
4. Serve with Greek yogurt and enjoy.

----*Afternoon Snack*----

10 peanuts will be enough to keep you going until dinner time.

----*Dinner*----

Mediterranean Chicken and Orzo

Preparation time->10 minutes

Cooking time->50 minutes

Ingredients:

- Lemon juice
- Virgin olive oil
- 3 oregano (dry)
- Coriander 2 Tsp
- 3teaspoons paprika
- Pepper and salt
- 7 garlic
- 4 cups of Chicken broth
- Whole Grain
- Tomatoes

Cooking instructions

1. Heat the oven on medium heat.
2. Pick a bowl and mix all the ingredient and spices together: coriander, pepper, paprika, salt, and oregano.
3. Add lemon juice to the coated chicken and set aside for 20 minutes.
4. Add chicken and cook for 10 minutes while flipping till they turn brown. Add green pepper.
5. In another oven, add ingredients: pepper, onions and olive oil together and cook while stirring for three minutes. Add chicken broth and salt and continue boiling.
6. Serve with Mediterranean salad and roasted garlic hummus.

Day 7

----*Breakfast*----

Creamy Blueberry and Pecan Oats

Preparation time-> 5 minutes

Cooking time-> 40 minutes

Ingredients:

- Pepper
- Garlic
- Olive oil
- Potatoes
- Onion
- Mixed herbs
- Tomatoes
- Egg
- Cheese

Cooking method

1. Heat the oven.
2. Boil water and put potatoes, let them boil for 8 minutes.
3. Prepare ingredients: pepper, cheese, onion, and tomatoes.
4. Fry the ingredients.
5. Add orange pepper and cook for a minute.
6. Cook potatoes with garlic for three minutes. Add cheese.
7. Beat eggs and drizzle garlic and pepper.
8. Pour the eggs on a vegetable mixture of cheese and bake for 20 minutes.
9. Serve while hot and enjoy.

----*Midmorning snack*----

Raspberry and Greek Yogurt

Preparation time->5 minutes

Ingredients:

- 2 tablespoon almonds (sliced)
- 2 cup raspberry
- ½ cup of Greek yogurt

Preparation method

1. Pick raspberry, mix Greek yogurt, and almonds then top with a raspberry.
2. Serve and enjoy.

----*Lunch*----

Tilapia

Ingredients:

- Tilapia

- Olive oil
- Butter
- Melon salsa

Cooking instructions

1. Heat olive oil and cook the tilapia at least 5 minutes while flipping.
2. Accompany the fish with mango-melon salsa, and a cup of strawberry Jell-O.
3. Serve and enjoy.

----*Dinner*----
Quinoa and roasted vegetables

Cooking time ->20 minutes

Ingredients:

- Vegetable and Quinoa
- Fudge bar and a side salad with vinaigrette or Italian dressing

Cooking instructions

1. Roast the vegetable and stir them together with quinoa.
2. Add fudge and a slide salad.
3. Serve them while hot.

Chapter 8: Mediterranean Diet Pyramid Chart

The pyramid was started as a means to help people have a planned diet and not a random dish at the table. The pyramid chart consists of the right outline of food expected to be eaten on the meal plan.

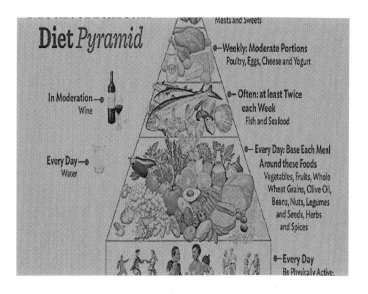

The chart was specially formulated based on diets of people with the longest lives living within the Mediterranean region. Studies show that what these people ate attributed their longevity. Essentially, the pyramid does not depict food quantities, but it is a general guideline on the foods that those long living adults ate. Additionally, it encourages communal eating as well as an active lifestyle.

It is linked with:

- Reduced chances of dementia and loss of memory
- Reduced chances of vascular diseases, stroke,and diabetes.

The meals are based on:

- Olive oil as the core source of fat
- Fruits and vegetables
- Whole grains, beans or legumes, and nuts

Important points to note (according to the chart):

- Take fish or seafood at least twice per week.
- Eat modest portions of poultry at least weekly or if possible daily.
- Take cheese, dairy, and eggs in sensible measures, at least weekly.
- For women, take one glass of wine per day, and for men, take two glasses per day.

The following foods should be eaten less often:

- Saturated fat
- Sweets
- Red meat
- Refined grains
- Highly processed foods
- Refined Oils
- Processed meat

More about the Mediterranean Diet Pyramid

In 1993, WHO, in conjunction with Harvard, developed the med diet Pyramid. Every now and then, researches are conducted on the pyramid and its benefits highlighted.

From the bottom of the pyramid, social relations and physical activity are emphasized. Moving up the pyramid, the major foods that you are supposed to buy are indicated. These foods include nuts, fruits, whole grains, olive oil, beans, nuts, spices, and vegetables.

Moving far up, you will realize that seafood and fish are normally taken two times a week. Dairy foods such as cheese and fermented dairy such as yogurt are taken more frequently but in moderate portions. Towards the top, you realize that poultry and eggs are highlighted. Sweets and meat are seldom eaten, and finally, wine and water are classic beverages.

The Mediterranean pyramid was created through intensified studies. According to pastresearch, it was discovered that the people living around the Mediterranean Sea were very healthy. They had a long life span rate compared to the death rate, unlike in other countries where people died at very early ages. After continued researches, it was discovered that the long-life aspect was not only attributed to the diet but also their lifestyle. Even those people living in the area, eating the region's foods without following any rules were still found very healthy. Another fascinating fact is that, even for the very old, their walking styles still remained intact. It took quite a very long time before they ended up in the wheelchairs; they had very strong bodies.

The pyramid is primarily considered as a lifestyle and not just as a restrictive diet. The reason behind this idea is because there is no specific meal plan attached to it. There is no specific time frame tohave a certain type of food for the day. When you compare the diet with the numerous modernized diets, some of them being fad diets, you will concur with me about the diet being a lifestyle. Those living around the region just ate a lot of seafood, veggies, nuts, and drank wine even on special occasions. This led to the diet as being an outstanding one. It influenced a lot of researches and people shifted from their areas to come and witness all they heard about the Mediterranean diet, and perhaps, become part of it.

All across the globe, the diet became very popular even due to some of its peculiar components. Some of those factors we had discussed earlier, but it breaks no bone to have a frisk overview of them, lest you forget. The populace of the region never took their meals in a rush; they took their time. They were oblivious of the fact that the move contributed positively to their health. Food was well-digested, and this countered stomach upsets. Also, taking food without haste reduced the risks of getting choked. Choking can lead to death since it blocks the windpipe and interferes with breathing.

Additionally, eating fast prompts taking huge portions of food. When you eat more food than your body requires, you outwardly develop obesity due to the accumulated fats. Previously, you learned about the effects of being overweight; they are very dire consequences indeed. All these odd constituents and a lot more others, made the Mediterranean diet home for people who were insatiably curious.

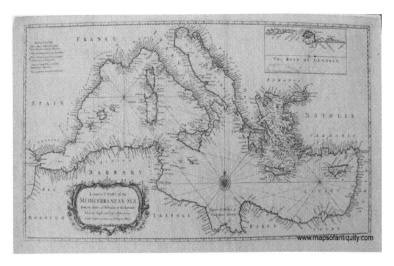

Mediterranean Location

The Mediterranean Seafood

According to the Med Diet pyramid chart, it shows that the diet reduces low-density lipoprotein (LDL). LDL is popularly known as 'bad cholesterol.' When low-density lipoprotein is reduced, the resultant effect is that the risks of Atherosclerosis condition are also warded off. The condition is a high risk one as it has been known to increase the death rate in the USA during the recent years. It is a major cause of heart attacks as well as strokes. The disorder brings about the narrowing of the arteries, also known as clogging of the arteries.

On an in-depth look at the med diet pyramid chart, you will find that the dietary patterns are connected with the reduction of chances of your offspringsbeing attacked by Spina Bifida. Spina Bifida can be defined as a congenital disability where the spinal cord is not fully developed, a condition that limits the mobility of children.

Columbian University conducted a study on the pyramid chart. The study revealed that, when you follow the chart to the latter, your chance of getting affected by Alzheimer's is greatly reduced by 40%.

Another study by the same institution showed that applying the chart to its finest details could reduce the risk of developing Parkinson's disease by approximately 50%. Through the study, the researchers revealed that eating meals with a high concentration of foods such as fruits, legumes, fish, and vegetables contributes to putting PD at bay. Taking foods that have low-fat saturation and avoiding red meat helps, too.

Further, according to the Mediterranean diet pyramid chart, the intake of food is highly regulated. The servings of vegetables, fruits, healthy fats (olive oil and healthy nuts) are done in moderation. Moreover, the intake of fish is highly increased while reducing the level at which red meat is consumed. You realize that alcohol consumption is also moderated.

Chapter 9: Bonus Recipes

Apart from the seven-day meal plan, there are other best choices for you to consider. The recipes below will be accompanied by a shopping list, a menu list, and ways of cooking the foods. The recipes will be based on certain scenarios like what to have for winter, for a wedding, for valentine, for holidays, or other special occasions as well as what's appropriate on a daily basis.

Shopping List

The shopping list is very important when it comes to cooking because it comes with a lot of benefits. The importance of the shopping list is that it helps avoid the last minute dash; rushing to the market to purchase food that you might have forgotten. Also, without a shopping list, you waste a lot of time wandering around the grocery shops aimlessly. A shopping list ensures you cook fresh foods. Having a shopping list will ensure that you reduce food wastages. When food wastages are eliminated, you save a lot of money as well.

Below is a list of what you should have in your kitchen before you even think of starting the cooking process. They are the ingredients of the Mediterranean Diet.

- Orange
- Apples
- Broccoli
- Spinach
- Kales
- Chicken
- Carrots
- Pepper
- Salt garlic
- Tuna
- Mackerel
- Brown rice

- Natural yogurt
- Lemmon for juice
- Almond
- Nuts
- Cashews
- Salmon

- Salad

- Peanut butter
- Eggs
- Grapes
- Wine
- Onions
- Olive oil

With such a list, you are good to go and set for cooking; it is also very important to make sure that you check your cooker for the right amount of fuel.

Let's dive into the various recipes.

1. Breakfast
This is known to be a light and a simple meal. You can choose the following for this level

Eggs for omelet or oatmeal

2. Snack
Fruits and Juice

3. Lunch
Vegetables and whole grains

4. Supper
Brown rice, salmon, tuna, chicken, poultry, or salmon

The above is just a sample of what you can have for your menu for the day. Beloware some recipes you can try out and means by which you can cook them.

Healthy Recipes To Have For Your Breakfast

Scrambled Eggs with Spinach

Talking of tasty and sweet, this is definitely the best choice for you. It is quick and the best for a romantic appeal.

Ingredients:

- Olive oil
- Pepper
- Salt
- Spinach (chopped)
- 2 eggs

How to cook

1. You first beat the eggs and whisk them in a bowl and then season them with salt and paper while still whisking them together.
2. Heat a saucepan till medium-high then add olive oil and place the eggs in the pan.
3. Add sliced spinach to the eggs and cook for 2 minutes while stirring and add a little salt to the mixture.
4. When done, serve with lemon juice and enjoy.

Egg muffins

Muffins are very sweet and make you feel fuller by the end of the breakfast. Below is the proper way of cooking.

Ingredients:

- Olive oil
- Salt and pepper
- Tomato spinach
- Bacon
- Mozzarella
- Garlic mushroom
- 2 eggs

How to Cook

- Heat the saucepan, add olive oil, and place peeled onion in it.
- Pick a bowl and beat 2 eggs on it while mixing with salt and pepper.
- Put the mixture to the frying pan and stir them together.
- Cook for 2 minutes then serve and enjoy.

Tostadas for breakfast

Are you a fan of homemade meals, someone who loves to cook and bake all the time? Then, it is definitely the best option for you.

Ingredients:

- Tortillas
- Foil
- Olive oil
- Refried beans (warmed)
- Grated sharp cheddar cheese
- Eggs
- Pico de gallo

How to cook

1. Preheat your oven – 400 degrees.
2. Place the baking sheets.

3. Pick a foil and spread it out then add the tortillas corn to it while spreading.
4. Spread oil on top of it while making sure you also sprinkle salt.
5. Make dough while rubbing it gently to the hands.
6. Bake tortilla till it turns golden- set it aside.
7. Prepare the re-fried beans, eggs, and pico de gallo.
8. When done, put to heat for baking and see to it that they become crispy.
9. On top of each tostada, place the re-fried beans.
10. Sprinkle with cheese and the eggs.
11. Spread picode gallo on the eggs.
12. Serve when hot and enjoy.

Mediterranean Cauliflower Salad

When talking of salad, vegetables are the first thing that comes to the mind. It is true that salad comes with a good amount of greens.

Ingredients:

- Cucumber
- Olive oil
- Cauliflower
- Onion
- Parsley
- Garlic
- Lemmon for juice

How to cook

1. Make juice out of lemon through grating.

2. Beat cauliflower in a bowl until it becomes rice-like.
3. Turn on the microwave and place the cauliflower in the microwave for about 6 minutes.
4. Pour the other ingredients of pepper, salt, oil, and garlic to the lemon juice and mix them together till they blend.
5. Pour the mixture into the salad.
6. Serve while hot and enjoy.

Mediterranean toast

Have you ever tried a Mediterranean toast? If not, then you are missing out on a very sumptuous dish. The Mediterranean toast should be at the top of the list. It is simple and easy to prepare. It only takes 5 minutes, and you are done and ready to eat.

Ingredients:

- Salt
- Pepper
- Cheese
- Tahini
- Tomatoes
- Wheat bread

How to cook

1. You first start by toasting your bread.
2. Place cucumber and tomatoes at the top.
3. Sprinkle cheese to the toasted bread.
4. Add salt and pepper to it and enjoy.

Quinoa salad

If you love eating food that comes from trees, then this is the way forward. Quinoa comes from dry seeds, and they are very delicious.

Ingredients:

- Pepper
- Avocado
- Cheese
- Olive oil
- Salt

- Onion
- Cucumber
- Tomato
- Lime juice

How to cook

1. Pick a bowl big enough for the ingredients and place them all there: cucumber, salt, pepper, tomato, olive oil, avocado, onion, and cheese.
2. Make quinoa separately then add to the bowl and stir them well till they blend.
3. Mix them all when done.
4. Serve with lime juice when done and enjoy.

Quinoa and Egg Muffin

Ingredients:

- Pepper
- Cheese
- Onion
- Eggs
- Oregano
- Spinach water
- Garlic

How to cook

1. Mix water with quinoa, place to heater pan and cook for 8 minutes making sure it is not fully cooked.
2. In another pan, cook onion for one 1 minute then add spinach.
3. Prepare muffin and bake for 20 minutes.
4. Mix the ingredients or follow step 1 and 2 with the remaining ingredients in the menu.
5. Serve while hot when done.

Shakshouka

Ingredients:

- Cumin seeds
- Olive oil
- Onions
- Pepper
- Garlic
- Tomato
- Parley
- Eggs
- Yogurt

How to cook

1. Preheat oven for medium heat.
2. Add olive oil and onions and cook for 30 seconds, then add tomatoes and salt plus pepper, then stir the mixture together till they blend.
3. Sprinkle cumin on top and cook for 10 minutes while tasting.
4. Add water after 5 minutes and taste to make sure it does not get dry.
5. After the 10 minutes,beat2eggs,whisk them, and pour them to the pan after making a hole to the mixture.
6. Cook for another 5 minutes.
7. Serve while hot and enjoy when done.
8. You can accompany with natural yogurt for complete menu.

8 Recipes for Snacks You Should Definitely Try

Fig and Honey Yogurt

Ingredients:

- Brown sugar
- Butter (melted)
- Natural yogurt
- Honey
- Fig

How to Prepare

1. Heat pan over medium heat.
2. Smear the figs with butter all over.
3. Sprinkle the sugar on both sides.
4. Cook for five minutes till brown.
5. Cool for a minute when done.
6. Drizzle figs with honey.
7. Serve with yogurt.

Cucumber Hummus and Sandwich

Ingredients:

- Hummus
- Pepper
- Lemon
- Cucumber
- Salt
- Oat bread

How to cook

1. Pick a bowl, slice the cucumbers and place them there then you can go ahead and sieve.
2. Add salt and pepper to the cucumber and drain them for 25 minutes.
3. Using a sharp thick knife, slice the lemon and throw the seeds or in another bowl.
4. Cut the bread into two equal halves and smear hummus all way to the bread while adding a little seasoning.
5. Smelt the cucumber slices with hummus of bread.
6. Make the sandwich with the bread slices and cut them diagonally for a great look.
7. Serve when done.

Roasted Red Hummus

Ingredients:

- Extra virgin olive oil
- Lemon juice
- Tahini
- Pepper
- Salt
- Water
- Paprika
- Garlic
- Chickpeas
- Red bell pepper

Cooking instruction

1. Drain chickpeas after soaking.
2. Simmer the chickpeas with salty water.
3. Drain the beans too and cool later.
4. Make sure to drain all of them for almost 2 hours.
5. Peel the chickpeas when done to make the hummus creamy.
6. Combine the chickpeas with the other ingredients: olive oil, lemon juice, tahini, pepper, and spices.
7. Cook for 10 minutes again.
8. Serve when done and enjoy.

Vegan Bistro

Ingredients:

- Whole Wheat
- Hummus
- Olive oil
- Cucumber
- Bell pepper
- Fresh Dill
- Pepper salt
- Almond
- Toothpick

Cooking method

1. Heat the oven with average heat.
2. Stuff the dates with 3 almonds.
3. Use toothpicks to make sure that the almonds are secured.
4. Bake the dates for 20 minutes and serve while hot.

Lemon Ricotta Honey Toast with Figs and Pistachios

Ingredients:

- Lemon juice
- Ricotta
- Bread
- Honey

- Figs
- Pistachio
- Lemmon zest

Cooking method

1. The first thing is to take the bread and put it in the toaster for toasting.
2. Wrap the ricotta together and put figs on top of it.
3. When done with the toaster spread the ricotta with the figs (sliced).
4. Sprinkle with pistachio when done with all the pieces.
5. Serve with lemon juice when done.

Tomato and Mozzarella

Ingredients:

- Basil leaves
- Tomatoes
- Mozzarella cheese
- Pepper and salt
- Balsamic vinegar
- Olive oil

Cooking method

1. Cut the tomato, mozzarella, and basil together and apply the same on the other ingredients.
2. Sprinkle with salt and pepper.
3. Pick a bowl, pour the vinegar and oil there, then sprinkle pepper and salt to it and mix well till they blend.
4. Mix the two together and serve when done.
5. Enjoy.

Raspberry Oatmeal

Ingredients:

- Milk
- Water
- Teaspoon
- Raspberry
- Oil
- Oats
- Maple syrup
- Raspberry jam

How to cook

1. Heat oven of medium heat.
2. Mix water, salt, and milk together.
3. Add oats as it continues to cook after three minutes.
4. Stir the mix together.
5. Cooking for 5 minutes and stir with brown sugar.
6. Lastly, you can drizzle with maple syrup.
7. Serve and enjoy.

8 Lunch Recipes You Should Try Out

Chicken and Rice

Ingredients:

- Chicken breasts
- Onion
- 2 tomatoes
- Rice
- Water

How to cook

1. Heat the cooking pot with medium heat.
2. While on it, slice and peel the onions and tomatoes.
3. Throw the onions to the cooking pot after adding oil and stir.
4. Add tomatoes to the solution after one minute.
5. While on it, boil the water.
6. Add the chicken breast to the hot cooking pot and add a little water and cook for 10 minutes on each side while turning.
7. On another pan, add oil, water, and salt then stir.
8. Add rice to the solution and stir.
9. Cook for 10 minutes.
10. Put the chicken and the rice in one plate.
11. Serve and enjoy.
12. You can serve with juice.

Kale and Feta Salad

This is very simple to cook and takes less time to cook, preparation, and cooking takes approximately 10 minutes for everything.

Ingredients:

- Pumpkin seeds
- Ounces
- 1 onion
- ½ cup of virgin olive oil
- Kale
- Lemon

Cooking method

1. Heat saucepan.
2. Throw the pumpkin into the pan and stir.
3. Make sure after the end of the 6 minutes, the seeds are lightly brown.
4. Blend the rest: onion, kale, and feta in a bowl.
5. Add all the other ingredients into the mixture.
6. Serve while hot and enjoy.

Chicken Pasta Salad

Ingredients:

- Minced onions
- Celery
- Cheddar cheese
- Mushroom
- Rotini
- Green olive frozen corn
- Mayonnaise
- Chicken Meat
- Italian style
- Bell pepper
- salt

How to cook

1. Bring the pot to fire and boil water (salted).
2. Add pasta and cook for 9 minutes.
3. Blend all the other ingredients together: olive, onion, mushrooms, cheese, corn, pasta, and peer.
4. Mix with the chicken for 1 hour.
5. Serve while hot.
6. Enjoy with lime juice.

Beef Stew

This is one of the most loved choices of meal, especially with the fact that it is very sweet and tasty. The aroma alone will make you starve.

Ingredients:

- virgin olive oil
- onions
- garlic
- water
- tomatoes
- pepper
- beef
- salt
- potatoes
- peas

How to cook

1. Chop all the available ingredients: onions, garlic, tomatoes, potatoes, and garlic.
2. Cut the beef into pieces.
3. Heat oil and cook the onion then add beef after a minute.
4. Stir for three minutes then add water after a few minutes, then continue cooking till the beef gets tender in shape.
5. Add salt after that. Add tomatoes after few minutes and mix them with garlic until the tomatoes become tender like the beef while stirring.
6. Add a little seasoning and continue stirring and cook for 5 minutes.
7. Serve while hot with some chapattis.

Turkey

They are big and very sweet. People love turkey because they are well-known for having fewer bones and a lot of meat. If you are very hungry, then this would help you a lot to satisfy your hunger. If you love cooking and you are not in a rush, try this out. It really works well. preparation and cooking take about 4 hours.

Ingredients:

- onion
- turkey
- salt
- celery
- pepper
- butter
- rosemary

How to cook

1. Heat pan with medium heat.
2. Cut and peel onions and carrots and place them on the pan.
3. Put the turkey gently on the pan and cook for 10 minutes.
4. Add pepper and salt and a little water and continue cooking while flipping the turkey.
5. In another pan, you can melt butter and cook it with rosemary for 2 minutes.
6. When done after the two minutes, place the rosemary inside the turkey.
7. Bake the turkey now for an hour or so.
8. Serve when hot and enjoy when done.

Greek Lentil Soup

Lentil soups are traditionally based. They are like herbs. They are best for curing the stomach, especially for pregnant women to help them gain energy. It takes about 1 hour 30 minutes and you are set.

Ingredients:

- Olive oil
- Onion
- Oregano
- Minced
- Garlic
- Pepper
- Carrot
- Carrot
- Tomato paste
- Leaves
- Dried rosemary
- Pepper
- Oil olive
- Vinegar

How to cook

1. Bring into heat and add water. Let it boil for 15 minutes.
2. Add olive oil and other ingredients: carrots, garlic, onion, and pepper, then you can stir after that.
3. Add the rest of the ingredients after 2 minutes: oregano, rosemary, leaves, and cover.
4. Season with pepper and salt after that and stir.
5. Let it cook for 1 hour while still stirring while adding a small amount of water.
6. Lastly, add vinegar when almost done.
7. Serve while hot.

Moroccan Soup

Moroccan soup is also traditionally based and founded in Morocco.

Ingredients:

- Olive oil
- Onions
- Carrots
- Minced
- Cumin
- Cinnamon
- Coriander
- Pepper
- Turmeric
- Chicken broth
- Water
- Tomato
- Cauliflower
- Spinach
- Cilantro

How to cook

1. Heat the oil.
2. Cut and peel onions and carrots all together and stir for 15 minutes.
3. Add water, tomato, and cauliflower to the pan then boil it until they become tender.
4. Cook for 10 minutes while stirring.
5. Serve with lemon juiced.

Beef Barley Soup

Ingredients:

- Olive oil – one tablespoon
- Beef chuck roast – 3 pounds
- Sweet onion – I large and chopped
- Carrots – two cups(sliced)
- Celery – two cups (sliced)
- Garlic (minced) – 4 cloves
- Beef broth – twelve cups
- Tomatoes – 1 can – 15 ounces
- Dried barley – 1 cup
- Thyme leaves - teaspoon
- Rosemary leaves – 1 teaspoon
- Red pepper – half teaspoon – crushed
- salt

<u>Instructions</u>

1. Take large sauce pot and heat (medium).
2. Put olive plus onions.
3. Sauté the onions – cook for three minutes.
4. Stir celery, garlic, and carrots – cook for five minutes.
5. Cut the beef into half-inch chunks.
6. Add the meat.
7. Cook until brown – five minutes – stir thrice.
8. Add tomatoes, herbs, red pepper, broth, barley. and salt (half teaspoon), then stir.
9. Cover until they boil.
10. Lower the heat.
11. Simmer until the beef is tender and barley is cooked.
12. Keep on stirring for 30 min.
13. Add salt and pepper to taste.

Mediterranean Diet for Dinner

Walnut and Salmon

Ingredients:

- California walnuts (one-half cup)
- Dijon mustard
- Salt and pepper
- Salmon fillets (three ounces)
- Virgin olive oil (one-half tablespoon)
- Breadcrumbs (three tablespoons)
- Lemon rind (three tablespoons)

Cooking Instructions

1. Place the nuts in the food processor and chop.
2. Mix the lemon rind and olive oil. Mix them well and add pepper and salt.
3. Spread the salmon fillets on baking sheets and brush the tops with Dijon mustard.
4. Spread the walnut mixture on each of the fillets.
5. Cover the fillets using plastic wrap.
6. Put them in the fridge for two hours.
7. Bake for twenty minutes on 350°F.
8. After they are ready, serve after sprinkling with lemon juice.

Mediterranean Diet for Special Occasions

Most weddings are fun, in fact, all weddings are fun. But when they involve evening parties, they become more fun than ever. The guests are left with memories that are edged in their memories for a lifetime. In these evening parties, dinner is obviously inevitable.

Mediterranean chicken orzo

Ingredients:

- One half pounds chicken thighs – boneless and skinless
- Sodium chicken broth – two cups
- Two Tomatoes – chopped
- Pitted green olives – one cup
- Pitted ripe olives – one cup
- Carrot – one piece and finely chopped
- One onion – chopped
- Lemonzest – one tablespoon grated
- Lemon juice – three tablespoon
- Butter – two tablespoon
- Herbs de Provence – one tablespoon

- Orzo pasts – uncooked one cup

Cooking Instructions

1. Heat the oven on medium heat.
2. Combine all the first eleven ingredients.
3. Cook while covered.
4. Cook until vegetables, chicken, andpasta become tender.
5. Add orzo in the last thirty minutes.
6. Serve while still warm.

Cucumber Hummus and Sandwich

Do you want to surprise your girlfriend or boyfriend on valentines? Let them wake up to a special sweet smell and delicious meal that is prepared in a simple way but can be used to show love to the partner.

Ingredients:
- Hummus
- Pepper
- Lemon
- Cucumber
- Salt
- Oat bread

How to cook

1. Pick a bowl, slice the cucumbers and place them there, then you can go ahead and sieve.
2. Add salt and pepper to the cucumber and drain them for 25 minutes.
3. Using a sharp thick knife, slice the lemon and throw the seeds to the dustbin in another bowl.
4. Cut the bread into two equal halves and smear hummus all way to the bread with a little seasoning.
5. Smelt the cucumber slices with hummus of bread.
6. Make the sandwich with the bread slices and cut them diagonally for a great look.
7. Serve when done.

Moroccan soup

Moroccan soup will make you relocate to the Mediterranean region. Moroccan soup does not only make the med diet popular but also improves your health significantly. Here is how to go about it.

Ingredients:

- Olive oil – one tablespoon
- Onion – one piece (chopped)
- Celery sticks – chopped
- Ground cumin – two tablespoon
- Hot vegetable stock – 600ml
- Tomatoes- can with garlic – 400ml
- Chickpeas – 400grams
- Broad beans – 100grams
- Zest and juice – half lemon
- Coriander
- Flatbread
- pepper

How to cook

1. Heat the oil in a saucepan.

2. Fry the onion and then the cumin.

3. Turn up the heat and cook the chickpeas, stock, and tomatoes.

4. Add pepper(ground) and simmer – 8min.

5. Put broad beans plus lemon juice.

6. Season to taste.

7. Sprinkle with zest.

8. Serve with flatbread.

Artichoke and oregano

You should definitely try this meal out because of its sumptuous taste. It is also very easy to prepare the dish; it takes just a few minutes. The dish was prepared during special occasion such weddings. In modern times the meal is preferred during engagement parties. Here is how to prepare it.

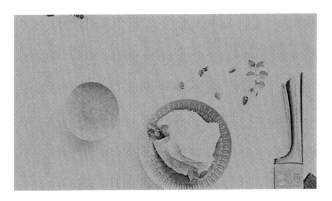

Preparation time ->10 minutes

Cooking time->20 minutes

Ingredients:

- 1 tablespoon Salt garlic
- 3 Olive oil
- Tomatoes
- 1 jar Artichoke hearts (chopped)
- 2 tablespoon Basil fresh
- 6 ounces of cheese and ice cream
- 2 tablespoon oregano
- Gnocchi 1 package

Cooking instructions

1. Heat olive oil in a pan.

2. Add sauté and salt until golden.

3. Add ingredients: artichokes, tomatoes, basil, and oregano.

4. Boil for 7 minutes.

5. Put half-size water in a pan, then add gnocchi and boil until you start seeing it float.

6. Stir all of them until they are fully combine for about 7 minutes.

7. Serve while hot and enjoy.

For any budding chef, or even an amateur cook, the importance of having a recipe in place is theoretical as well as practical. A recipe shows the technical part of a dish. It teaches the typical and the artistic blend of texture and taste of any meal. A recipe depicts the ingredients or components of a meal. Apart from ingredients, it also shows the procedures for preparing a particular meal. A detailed recipe will show the time frame of preparing the meals.

Here are the five parts of a recipe:

1. Yield – This part shows the sizes of servings. It tells you whether you need less or additional food.

2. List of Ingredients – Shows the components needed to prepare a meal.

3. Procedure – Shows the steps for preparing the meals.

4. Equipment – List of cooking equipment that you will require while preparing the meals.

5. Temperature and time – This part shows the temperature needed to cook certain foods. It also

shows the duration of time required to cook different types of foods.

Conclusion

Having made it to this far is a definite sign that you have been reading this informative eBook. Thank you for taking the time to read it right from the beginning through to its end. Congratulations also for making that brilliant step to try to beat the biggest dilemma known to humans: dieting.

In contrast to the numerous diets available globally, the *Mediterranean Diet for Beginners* has been designed in a heart-healthy way. It is basically intended for you as a starter, to help you try new foods while still training your body to adopt natural foods as opposed to processed foods.

Since you have now read the book and you have a crystal clear glimpse on how to start on the Mediterranean diet, it is time to make a move. Start from the basics, skip the myths you have ever heard about the Med diet, you already are enlightened about the dreadful diseases, so follow the meals to the latter. Go slow on the exercises, and eventually, you won't go wrong on the diet, you will always feel great!

The Mediterranean Diet is not static, but it is rather fluid. It is prone to modifications and adjustments upon on-going researches. So, when you expect that this book will offer all that you need to know about the diet as a beginner, I bet, you are expecting too much. There are many, many conferences out there held about the Mediterranean diet, attending one of them sounds like a whir of activity. You will learn more in addition to what you have learned from this book. You will realize that change doesn't come overnight, it takes time.

So, there is nothing to wait. Go Mediterranean and start your journey towards a healthy lifestyle!

If you've found this book helpful in any way, a review on Amazon is very much appreciated and if you liked it you might also like:

THE MEDITERRANEAN DIET PLAN

(Book 2)

INTRODUCTION

Congratulations for viewing this book *The Mediterranean Diet Plan: Your Daily Guide to Healthy Eating with a 4-Week Meal Plan, Tips and Tricks for Successful Weight Loss and Nutritious Mediterranean Recipes*. This book is a guide aimed at achieving a healthy life for you and your family. It primarily points out how you can live a life free from nutritional ailments as well as from the hassles associated with budgeting. Enjoy your time going through it and get educated as well.

The following chapters delve more on the Mediterranean diet as well as how they are prepared. They also point out possible solutions and tips on how to lead a healthy life as well as to have enjoyable meals. The aim of this book being written was to educate, empower, and motivate you to get out of that comfort zone and push your limits in an adventurous manner. This information does not hold a final word on diets but is one that can be relied on and followed. The book helps from the typical person to the busiest of individuals on how to live life in a well cut out manner, stalking and tethering you in wellness. Through extensive research and comparison from reliable and credible sources, this book provides relevant information about the topics.

As you peruse through, take notes, steal ideas or two, try new recipes, and be informed on the key things and principles that could affect you in one way or another. However, the duplication or transmission of any of the information provided will be considered illegal and irrespective. The content in this book is of informative purposes only. To the reader, props for choosing your ultimate guide to health, have fun!

CHAPTER1: HEALTHY EATING

Healthy eating is primarily the consumption of a vast choice of foods that provide you with essential nutrients for proper growth and sate wellbeing. These vital nutrients comprise of minerals and vitamins, proteins, carbohydrates, and fats and oils. When properly put together in quantitative portions, it forms a balanced diet which is considered the only healthy meal choice.

Examples of such foods include:

- Fruits and vegetables—kales, mangoes, oranges, spinach
- Healthy fats—low-fat milk, omega-3, olive oil
- Seafood—fish
- Animal produce—meat
- Whole grain—cereals, rice

Importance of Proper Nutrition

Well, healthy eating has always been attributed to proper food choices as they affect your daily lives in all ways. Have proper meals which are nutritious and healthy always.

Whether you're on some workouts or out on a quest for a healthy life, it is always good to feed both your soul and body with what's essential and beneficial. When you epitomize the principles and philosophies of healthy eating, the chances of falling prey to chronic illnesses are cut by half to none at all. This promotes your health as a whole as well as your lifestyle.

Below are some of the importance:

- **Passes Healthy Virtues for the Next Generation**

If you are a parent or guardian, well basically, the children and younger ones depend on you for everything. So, why don't you lay them a firm and healthy foundation as they grow according to your ways? Trade on that straight path because these people are looking up to you.

- **Mood Elevation**

When you're properly fed, you're happy, but when you're well fed and fully healthy, the feeling is priceless. Chances of suffering from depression or getting frustrated either financially or physically are null in such a case.

- Nutritious diets give you a longer life.
- Risks of lifestyle ailments are reduced.
- Strengthens your immune system.
- Enables you to manage and maintain your weight.

Tips for a Healthy Diet

Well, it's not rocket science, and basically, anyone with a sober mind can be able to undertake this. You just need food, discipline, and good consistency levels if you want to achieve healthy living.

Various ways of improving your diet include:

- Replacing sugary drinks with water of fresh fruit juice.
- Reducing meat intake or rather quantitating its consumption.
- Always have a balanced diet, incorporate much of those greens.
- Prefer whole grain or fresh produce to process foods.
- Roast more than you fry to cut off the excess oils and fats.
- Always be open to new diets and healthy meals—open-minded and flexible.
- Avoid skipping meals.
- Have a workable meal plan.
- Don't be too hard on yourself but remain disciplined.

With a whole load of them, we could go all day long but most importantly set goals and work towards achieving them. It's also advised to seek a dietitian's help and advisory services

CHAPTER 2: FOUR-WEEK MEAL PLAN AND HOW TO PREPARE

Introduction to a Meal Plan

A meal plan is just as it is, plans for meals. Well, this is not a complex procedure or operation that really involves a diet. It is just a strategic and precise way meals can be prepared and taken for a futuristic end goal of a healthy lifestyle. It requires a bit of detail into it as well as proper planning, extensive research, maybe consultation from a dietitian, and adequate time. Meal plans cover all food timetables, all from main course meals to day to day snacks. A meal plan is set to help save a lot, in terms of expenses, time and even a lot of unnecessary thinking.

Meal planning is one of the easiest things to do as long as you know what you want at the end of it. To set you for a healthy course, one should, however, delve more in nutritious foods and check in what proportions they should be taken and with a blend of what. Be it monthly, weekly, biweekly, or all year long, the choice is yours. You can do it for your family, yourself, or even for an institution.

For a meal plan to be considered functional, there are factors that have to be put in place. One has to be disciplined and self-driven. You cannot set up a meal timetable for yourself and expect someone to push you into living by it. Whether you're setting up a meal for weight issues, health issues, or just for a healthy lifestyle, you're required to be motivated by yourself and know what goals you're planning to achieve. Meal plans are mostly found in schools because of the time that it saves.

Tips for a Successful Meal Plan

Always Refer to Your Meal Plan

For you to have a meal, you require to know what you are to cook, and for you to know what to cook, you require a meal plan. A meal plan helps you check on your schedule and plan out your day or week beforehand to avoid inconveniences. It also shows you what you need for certain meals, how to prepare them as well as in what quantities. You may be someone with a busy schedule and most at times ends up having nights out either because you have no idea on what to eat or are just tired. Well, it happens to most of us during specific times that were not in a position to cook. We end up having foods that are unhealthy all in the name of saving time and energy. With a meal plan in place, you need not to worry on what you can eat all because it comes in as an automated kitchen helper that has all you need and can help you get the job done.

Have a Journal

A journal? Well, yes, have a journal. It is essential and comes in handy. With the exploration of new foods and ideas that you can't store all in your mind, you have to remember you're prone to forgetting. It helps you keep an account of what is to be done besides having your meal plan. You can keep secret surprise recipes for your loved ones, meals that you have cooked in the past that everybody loved. It is a good way to remember things; considering someone with a lot going on, you'll have no choice but to pen down something. Constantly, with new ideas streaming in for your dietary, you can't squeeze them in your meal plan. Jot them down and have them as a bag of extra tricks up your sleeve. It will inspire you as you even add up to information in it showing you your journey from where it all started till where you are currently, encouraging more reason to forge on with your quest for good health.

Come Up with Theme Nights

There is always that one thing that all your people will enjoy taking. Coming up with a theme night for food will not only push for that healthy lifestyle but also make everyone always anticipate for the day. Expectations always bring about profound joy and happiness, and this is lone recipe for it. It may work for all of the people in your home, but coming up with theme night could help a lot. If it is someone's favorite dish being prepared, you can be sure of getting a helping hand. Your family will get more involved as well as you will get a chance to bond and share the importance of healthy eating. You will be getting suggestions on how to prepare the specific meals, how they are best prepared and have the whole ordeal tether you and your family around a healthy lifestyle.

Get Something to Inspire You

Why do you have a meal plan in the first place? What made you come up with one? Why are you even on a healthy diet in the first place? Those are some of the things that you are supposed to ask yourself as you are on this journey. Your family could be your sole motivation, probably because you don't want them to end up like your neighbor's kids, all chubby and obese. Maybe it is you who don't want to die of an illness caused by an unhealthy lifestyle and leave your family behind. Get that one thing that inspires you to be a better person, to always go a mile ahead as well as push the limits all for the greater good—a healthy life. Inspiration is all around you; just keep a keen eye and ear and meditate in what your soul will lead you to. Funny how food matters can end up spiritual huh.

Have a Plan for All of a Day's Meal

A meal plan essentially covers every meal in a day. It's your duty to see to it that meals one needs to eat are catered three times a day. If you don't plan them out, you are prone to go out and have meals from taken away joints or restaurants and lose track of your healthy eating. You are more likely to also skip meals as well as starve which is inconvenient to your body in one way or another. In this way, you can formulate ways that you can make quick and easy healthy meals in case of someone being in a hurry. Incorporate snacks too in your meal plan. They are the ultimate saviors when one is not in moods for a plate of rice or mashed potatoes.

Know Everyone's Preference and Specialties

Well, we are all different and not everyone eats what we eat. To avoid cooking food that will only remain in the serving dish, seek to know what your people or someone likes. People react differently to different foods, and you'd not want to be the cause of someone's stomach ache or allergies. Meal planning will help you save the time of wondering what to cook that will be consumed by everyone. Some are just picky eaters, and some are just spoilt and for whatever reason won't have what you're serving for dinner. Some are just unfamiliar to some foods and require some time to adjust. So having separate quick recipes to accommodate the odd, ones would be of great help as well and will make the other party not to feel like you're shoving greens down their throats. In all of it, keep in mind our quest for a healthy lifestyle.

Make Everyone Involved

Having that extra hand has always been proven helpful. When everyone is involved, they get a glimpse of what happens each and every time before they are served with that pasta. This gives you, the dietician in the house, a chance to spread your gospel of healthy eating. You can innovatively turn the venture into a way of teaching on the nutritional value of some foods and their importance in the body. Getting involved does not only circle around the kitchen counter but also one can get involved by going for things in the supermarket or grocery store. The more active they are, the more they will feel part of the healthy eating revolution. When everyone is involved, it's a sure bet that everyone will eat and enjoy. A meal collectively prepared is full of love and with a touch of perfection.

Have a Planned Schedule

Living a random life is one way of living a confused life in other words. As a meal plan will plan out your dietaries, you should, however, plan out your life. Not like the whole of it but always review your daily activities and have them synced with your meal plan. This will prevent activities or events from colluding and open doors to meal compromise. A schedule will help you know where you're supposed to be and what you're supposed to be doing. It's more like a mini-manager that always has your daily accounts and guides you so that you walk in the right path. At times, things get out of hand and some things just can't be reversed or avoided, well, it's understandable, we are all humans. But that shield is not to be a loophole to invite unhealthy eating habits. You can always have a cheat meal, but make it healthy.

Keep Records

Having gone a full month on a diet plan, you'll be having some experiences as well a whole lot of recipes in your journal. When you keep records, you are able to know which type of food came out as the all-time favorite and which meal you worked your wits off and made it a success. I mean just have records of your time in the process. Those things when looked at or read, you feel motivated and empowered. Records also help you keep track of your expenditure all across the month and evaluate what changes need to be applied or implemented. With records, you can always pull that copy-paste method of doing thing so that you get the same results or experience you had. Before you are even aware, you'll have a load of ideas and reference points to check in case of anything.

Stay Organized and Label

It is not quite hard to distinguish things in the kitchen. I mean you can call lean meat carrots or vice versa. When it comes to the small details in a dietician's kitchen, you have to keep things organized and well labeled. This keeps out chances of confusing spices or tools of the arts. Keeping a tidy kitchen counter makes things easily available and visible, hence promotes a sense of easy workability. The same way as you have your meal plan planned out in a systematical order, have your kitchen as well as tools of the trade. This will keep you on track even as you carry out your operations, be it cooking or planning out a meal.

Have Your Meal Plan Beside Your Shopping List

As you check on what we are having for supper, you also need to check what we need to buy. Having your shopping list strategically placed helps you see what you miss or what you require to make a meal a success. There is nothing more disappointing than starting on a meal, then when you're already half-way into it, you notice some missing ingredients. It leaves everything frustrated and messed up as well as wasted.

Work on Perishables First

As we all know, perishables are basically fresh vegetables or rather fruits. They have a pretty short shelf life, hence they cannot be kept for long. While some tend to remain fresher for longer periods, it's wise to first consume them and have more room for fresher produce. The fresher they are, the more nutritious and healthy they are for consumption.

Buy Only What You Need

We all have, at some point, ended up buying something we did not want or need. Keenly looking into that matter, you'll notice that you didn't have a shopping list in place. As you go to buy stuff, have a list with you. This will save you both money and time. At the same time, buy conclusively. I mean make sure you buy all you need to avoid situations where you have to go back. When you directly go for what you want, unnecessary items will find their way into your cart. Don't be too hard on yourself but spend wisely. Focus on your needs not wants.

Always Ask for Feedback

Each time you cook a meal, ask on how a second or third party likes it. Have them criticize it in one way or another. If a meal turns out golden, well thumbs up, way to go our royal chef! However, if the feedback comes otherwise, know where to rectify and improve on. This will make you please everyone as well as delight in your cooking. It is one way to boost your self-esteem as you flaunt your cooking prowess in your palace—kitchen.

Bring Up Surprise Dishes

With a lot of exotic healthy meals from the Mediterranean, one can always have a new meal for the family, a surprise dish. You can always get one from cookbooks as well as from nutritionists. Of course, this is a venture for the adventurous and those willing to explore new tastes and recipes. Have it written down in your journal far from the meal plan accessible to all. This way, you will pull new tricks from time to time, and your next move will be unpredictable.

Always Have Your Meal Plan Written Down.

If you're planning to have it all in your head, I think you're just being comical. Who really has all those ingredients, measurements, nutrient content, and all the days of the year in their heads? Have your plan written down; you won't lose a tooth or a single strand of hair by just writing down your plan. This brings about a sense of responsibility as well as makes you accountable to follow on what you have written. It also helps you plan out your days as well as fix your schedules depending on what meals you are to cook that day. A meal plan written down will help you know what you need from the grocery store as well as the supermarket. Imagine relying on your busy mind and you get to forget a key ingredient of a meal, of which you can't cook without, how horrid. So, embrace that pen and paper and map out your weekly plan. Stay organized and stay focused.

Benefits of a Successful Meal Plan

Help You Save Money

With a meal plan, you already know what you want. That is in terms of purchasing and cooking. You won't be making the endless trips to the store trying to look for what you forgot or never found. This will keep you in line against impromptu expenditure on unnecessary items. As you also buy your items in bulk, you get chances on discounts which also add up to that saved amount. A meal plan will keep the few bucks you have in your pocket from ending up in a fast food joint cashbox or in take away orders. So pen that meal plan now and start a journey of health and wealth.

Saves You a Lot of Time

You'll take not more than a day to plan out your meal plan. This one day, in return, will save you lots of hours that could have been wasted strolling around the kitchen counter or gazing in front of a wide-open fridge trying to think of what to eat. As well, a meal plan saves you time at the grocery store, in that, you'll only be going there to specific sections, pick, go pay, and out you go. This keeps you from wandering in the store and yet finding yourself in the inner circles of shelves with unhealthy food items, that are always tempting. A meal plan will have you visiting the store only once or twice a week.

Keeps You on a Healthy Diet

Well, a meal plan is planning of diets. As you are planning on leading a healthy lifestyle, you'll have no other choice but to incorporate nutritious foods in your plan. A meal plan will ensure that you have no excuse to skip meals since every meal is already planned for and can be easily made. All week long, a meal plan has a perfectly crafted timetable that fits your schedule and slots you available for every meal, well unless otherwise. A meal plan, having all meals catered for, eliminates chances of you going for take away meals or night outs. You'll plan ahead as well as have home cooked meals, made by you, for you and for the greater good of a healthy lifestyle.

Reduces Food Wastage

Without a meal planner, you end up having things in excess and some you don't even need. You'll have three loaves of bread yet you only eat a half a loaf. That extra item always ends up as a substitute for another thus opening a doorway for wastage in one way or another. When going to the stores, you end up buying what you already have and have more of it, some being perishables of which won't see the day of light if not in a trash can. Foods will often time get spoilt in the cupboards or counters even before you have them put in the freezer all because of overstocking; some even lack space due to abundance. With a meal plan, you'll look at what you have and know what you are to add on. If there are any chances of leftovers, a meal plan will help you best deal with it to avoid wastage.

Helps Reduce Stress

Stress comes when you don't know what to eat yet you have all you need to fix a meal. Stress could also come as a result of confusion on what everyone likes or prefers taking at a specific time. Stress, again, comes when you have unhealthy eating habits. How? Well, when you gas up on junk foods and end up obese, you'll always be stressed and frustrated on who is checking you out. A meal plan comes in handy since it will help and organize you, both in your daily schedules as well as dietary. It helps put out a healthy choice of a meal that will be convenient and easy to prepare without complicated recipes. A meal plan will as well help you save up on stressful expenditures.

Shopping Becomes Easier

Finally, a meal plan keeps you organized and time cautious. As you plan ahead, you're also shopping for the same ahead. You'll be stocking up on the things that you'll need for the next month or a few weeks to come. You'll be entering that store and going precisely where your items of choice are, not aimlessly pushing that cart with no idea in mind.

How Does the Mediterranean Diet Works?

As we all know, the Mediterranean has a lot of cuisines to its name. The diet itself is curved out the lifestyle there. It came about naturally as the region provided the food. It has a vast lineage of healthy diets that one can live on and make out a meal plan out of. This is to both live a healthy lifestyle as well as enjoy the tantalizing rare dishes.

The region's diet is famously known for its nutritious meals all rich with flavor and benefits for one's body. The foods have been famously known to manage a variety of serious illnesses and lifestyle diseases. Adopting the Mediterranean diet can enable one to improve their health and live longer in a healthy lifestyle.

It's never really about the quantity but quality of food you partake. Below is a four-week meal plan from the Mediterranean diet. This will carry you through your weight loss program, keep you fit, and leave your taste buds happy.

WEEK 1 DIET PLAN

SUNDAY

Breakfast

Mediterranean Scrambled Eggs

Preparation Time is approximately 5 minutes, Cooking Time estimated at 10 minutes bringing a Total Time of 15 minutes

Ingredients

- 1 yellow pepper, diced
- 8 cherry tomatoes (quartered)
- 2 spring onions, sliced
- Black pepper
- 2 tablespoon sliced black olives
- 4 eggs
- 1 tablespoon of capers
- Oil (1 tablespoon)
- Oregano (1/4 teaspoon and dried)
- Fresh parsley, to serve (not a must)

Instructions

1. With oil heating inside the pan, put in the pepper as well as spring onions (chopped), let the oil become hot. With heat (medium), cook until it is slightly soft. Thereafter put in the Olives, capers your tomatoes then let them Cook for just a minute.

2. Scramble the eggs in the pan, put in the oregano and black pepper. Stir till the eggs are ready then serve with fresh parsley.

Nutrition

249 calories, 14g protein, 17g of fat, 334mg of sodium, 13g carbohydrates, 3g fibers, 4g of sugar

Lunch

Caprese Salad with Grilled Haloumi and Herbs

4 servings

<u>Ingredients</u>

- Salt and pepper (ground)
- Olive oil
- ½ lemon
- ½ pound of sliced cheese
- 5 torn leaves (basil)
- 1 pound of tomatoes (slice them into rounds)
- Flat-leaf parsley (2 tablespoons and finely chopped)

<u>Instruction</u>

1. Have medium-high heat on your grill.
2. Lightly squeeze some lemon over the tomatoes (arranged onto a plate) then season them using salt both with the pepper.

3. Apply oil on the grill grates then put the halloumi and start cooking, turning only once, until markings appear having the cheese warmed throughout, about, give each side a minute. Put on the tomatoes afterwards then Drizzle some olive oil on salad as well as the parsley and basil.

Nutrition

8g carbs, 196 calories, 6g sugars, 9g proteins, 15g fat

Dinner

Greek Turkey Meatball Gyro with Tzatziki

Preparation Time 10 minutes, Cooking Time 16 minutes bringing a Total Time 26 minutes

Components

Meatball:

- Red onions (¼ cup and finely chopped)
- Salt and some pepper for seasoning
- Garlic (2 cloves and minced)
- 1 lb. turkey (ground)
- Spinach(1 cup fresh and chopped)
- Oil (2 tablespoons of olive)
- Oregano (a teaspoon)

Tzatziki Sauce:

- Some salt to taste
- ¼ cup cucumber (grated)

- ½ cup of plain Greek yoghurt
- Lemon juice (2 tablespoons)
- 1 cup of diced tomatoes
- Dry dill (1/2 teaspoon)
- 4 whole wheat flatbreads
- garlic powder (a half teaspoon)
- Red onion(½ bowl thinly sliced)
- A cup of diced cucumber

Instructions

1. Put the diced red onions, ground turkey, minced garlic, salt oregano, pepper, and fresh spinach, and using your hands, mix them together until it starts to stick together.
2. Shape them into meatballs.
3. Have a large skillet hot at medium heat then put in some oil (olive) inside the pan then put in your meat balls. Cook every side in 3-4 minutes until, and when they appear brown, remove from the pan.
4. Put Greek yogurt in a bowl and mix together with garlic powder, grated cucumber, dill, lemon juice, and salt for taste.
5. On the flatbread, assemble the gyros then add the tomato, cucumber, sliced red onions, and the 3 meatballs. On top pour the Tzatziki sauce.

Nutrition

Cholesterol 91mg, Calories 429, fats 19g, proteins 28g, Sugar 4g,fiber 3g, sodium 630mg,carbohydrates 38g, saturated fat 3g

MONDAY

Breakfast

Watermelon, Feta, and Balsamic "Pizza"

Cooking Time = 15 minutes

<u>Ingredients</u>

- 1 oz crumbled Feta cheese
- 1 teaspoon of mint leaves
- 5 to 6 Kalamata Olives, sliced
- 1 watermelon slice, cut an inch from the center
- 1/2 tablespoon balsamic glaze

<u>Instruction</u>

1. Slice into half of the widest part of the melon then lay the flat side onto a board and slice an inch thick from each of the halves. Cut each half to 4 wedges.

2. Arrange them on a dish and add some mint leaves, balsamic glaze, cheese, and olives.

Nutrition Value

2g proteins, 90 calories, 12g sugars, 3g fat, 1g fiber, 14g carbs, 148mg sodium

Lunch

Stuffed Eggplant

A good one to carry to work!

Preparation of ten minutes, Cooking Time of forty minutes and a fulltime of fifty minutes

Four servings

Components

- Red onion (one and in dices)
- Garlic (two cloves and minced)
- Cremini mushrooms (one pint and quartered)
- Eggplants (two medium and in halves)
- Olive oil (three tablespoons and separated)
- Black pepper and salt (freshly ground)
- Greek yogurt (a half cup and plain)
- Parsley (three tablespoons fresh and chopped)
- Kale (two cups and torn)
- Quinoa (two cups and cooked)
- Thyme (one tablespoon fresh and chopped)
- One lemon (juice as well as zest) (have wedges)

Instructions

1. Have your oven at 400°. Get your baking pan lined with vellum paper.
2. Scoop the flesh out of your eggplant with a spoon. Transfer your eggplant to your baking paper after rubbing one and a half teaspoon of oil in every half of it.
3. Put a tablespoon of oil to your cooking pan and have it heated over moderate temperatures. Put in your onions

and have them sautéed till soft for three to four minutes. For an additional minute with some garlic in have it cooked till aromatic.

4. Put in your mushrooms and let them cook till soft for four to five minutes. Have your quinoa and kales stirred in and let the kales be cooked till slightly wilted for two to three minutes. Using thyme, pepper, salt, and lemon juice and zest have your mixture seasoned.

5. Having spooned the filling in your eggplant, let them roast till your eggplants are soft but firm in seventeen to twenty minutes then allow it for five minutes to cool.

6. Have your meal garnished using parsley and served together with lemon wedges and yoghurt.

Nutrition

46g carbs, 339 calories, 15g fat, 12g protein

Dinner

Crispy Salmon Greek Orzo

Servings—4

Preparation Time 10 min, Cook Time20 min

Ingredients

Salmon:

- Coconut oil (two tablespoon and melted)
- Two pounds salmon (about an inch thick)
- Lemon pepper (one teaspoon)
- Dill (one teaspoon and dried)

Orzo:

- ½ lemon, juiced
- ¼ mug red onion, diced
- Orzo pasta(one cup and dried)
- Olive oil(two tablespoons)
- One yellow pepper, chopped
- ½ mug feta cheese, crumbled
- Garlic (one clove and mince)
- Pepper and salt for tasting
- Tomato (one chopped)
- Cucumber (one cup and chopped)
- Olives(a half a cup and sliced)

Instructions

1. Have your broiler at high temperatures then get your rack adjusted that's near your oven. Put salmon onto the baking sheet, then brush the two sections using coconut oil

(melted) thereafter have lemon pepper sprinkled on top as well as dill. Grill it in four to five minutes each section till it's crispy.

2. Boil the pasta till cooked as per package's directions. While boiling, have the oil, garlic, juice (lemon) as well as pepper and sodium chloride (salt) whisked. In a bowl, put in the tomatoes, olives, onion, pepper (yellow) as well as cheese.

3. Get your pasta drained, go ahead and rinse using cold water, put inside the bowl having your veggies. Pour in the mixture (olive) on then combine by tossing. Have your orzo served together with lemon wedges and crispy salmon.

TUESDAY

Breakfast

Egg Muffins with Ham

Preparation Time of 10 minutes, Cooking Time of 15 minutes bringing a Total Time of 25 minutes

Servings—6

Components

- Red pepper (½ cup roasted and sliced)
- Spinach (1/3 cup), minced
- Feta cheese (¼ cup)—crumbled
- 9 slices of thin cut deli ham
- 5 large eggs
- Pinch of pepper
- Pinch of salt

- 1½ tablespoons of pesto sauce
- Fresh basil for garnish

Instructions

1. Heat your oven up to 400. Limitlessly spray your muffin tin using a spray for cooking.
2. Put your muffins inside the tin; do not leave holes, the egg mixtures will explode off.
3. Put red pepper (roasted) at the bottom of every tin.
4. Place minced spinach (1 tablespoon) on every red pepper.
5. Top the pepper and spinach off with a heaping ½ Tablespoon of crumbled feta cheese.
6. In a bowl (medium), whisk the eggs together with salt and some pepper. Put the egg combination equally in every tin.
7. Allow 15-17 minutes of baking until puffy.
8. Remove cup from tin and garnish with tomato sauce (¼ teaspoon), put in red pepper (roasted) and basil.

Nutrition

Calories 109, Carbohydrates 1.8g,Fat 6.7g, Polyunsaturated Fat of 0.9g,Fat(Monounsaturated) 1.7g, Fat(Saturated) 2.4g, Cholesterol 169mg, Potassium 60mg, Total Dietary Fiber 1.8g, Sodium 423mg, Sugar 1.2g, Protein 9.3g

Lunch

Grilled Lemon-Herb Chicken and Avocado Salad

Preparation Time 35 minutes, Cooking Time of 1 hour and a Total Time of 1 hr&35 minutes

4 servings

Components

Lemon-Herb Chicken

- 1½ pounds boneless, skinless chicken breasts
- Olive oil—extra virgin(3 tablespoons)
- 1 tablespoon chopped and fresh dill
- Parsley(3 tablespoons, fresh and chopped)
- 2 lemons (zest as well as juice)
- Salt (kosher) and black pepper(ground freshly)
- 1 tablespoon chopped fresh oregano

Salad

- 1 cup barley
- 1 lemon(zest as well as juice)
- Chicken broth (2 and a half cups)
- Whole-grain mustard(a tablespoon)
- Oregano(a tablespoon and dried)
- Olive oil(a third cup extra virgin)
- Salt(Koshar) and black pepper(ground freshly)
- Red-leaf lettuce (2 heads and chopped)
- Red onion (one halved in slices)
- 1-pint cherry tomatoes, sliced
- Avocados 2(sliced)

Instructions

Prepare the lemon, heat the chicken

1. Place the chicken inside a big sealable bag (plastic). In a bowl (medium-sized), whisk your olive oil together with the lemon zest and juice, oregano, dill, and the parsley. Have your dressing in a sealed bag then refrigerate for thirty minutes.

Make the salad

2. Meanwhile, in a medium saucepan, let them simmer(barley and chicken broth) in medium heat. When it simmers, cook until barley becomes tender, 35 to 45 minutes. Drain and reserve.
3. In a bowl (medium), whisk the lemon juice and zest together with the mustard and your oregano. Gradually

stream in oil (olive) and whisk properly to combine. Season with salt and pepper.

4. Prepare your grill for heat (high). Remove your chicken out of the marinade and season it with salt as well pepper.

5. Grill it and ensure it is ready and charred on each side. Flipping through, give 10 to 12 min. reserve the chicken afterwards.

6. Into a large bowl, add in together the lettuce, onion as well as tomatoes. Put in the dressing then toss properly to coat.

7. Slice your chicken then serve on top of your salad alongside the avocado.

Nutrition

Lemon-Herb Chicken

309 calories, 15g fat, 4g carbs, 39g protein, 1g sugars

Salad

602 calories, 36g fat, 60g carbs, 15g protein, 8g sugars

Dinner

Easy One Pan Mediterranean Cod

Preparation Time of 5 minutes, Cooking Time of 30 minutes bringing a Total Time of 35 minutes

Servings—4

Components

- Olive oil (two tablespoons)
- Fennel (two cups and sliced)
- 3 large cloves garlic chopped
- 1 cup diced fresh tomatoes
- 2 cups shredded kale
- A tomato (14 ounces canned and diced)
- A small onion sliced
- A cup oil-cured black olives
- Water (half a cup)

- Red pepper (a pinch and crushed)
- Oregano (two teaspoons and fresh) or a half teaspoon oregano and dried
- Black pepper(a quarter teaspoon)
- Salt (an eighth teaspoon—1/8)
- Fennel seeds(a quarter teaspoon) optional
- Orange zest (a teaspoon)
- A lb. cod cut into 4 portions
- 1/4 teaspoon fennel seeds optional
- Have garnish
- Oregano fennel fronds
- Orange zest
- Olive oil

Instruction

1. In a skillet with medium heat, start cooking the onion as well as fennel and garlic in olive oil for 8 minutes then season it with some salt and pepper (a quarter teaspoon of each). Add tomato (canned and diced), fresh tomatoes, the kale, water. Stir then cook for 12 minutes. Put in red pepper (crushed), fresh oregano, then olives.
2. Prepare the fish (seasoned with pepper, fennel seeds (optional) orange zest and salt. Nestle the fish in kale tomato mixture. Cookit for about 10 minutes.
3. Remove it from the heat, then finalize with fennel fronds, some fresh oregano, orange zest, then drizzle the olive oil on top.

Nutrition

Calories 257, Fat 13g, fat 1g (Saturated),Cholesterol 48mg,Sodium 700mg,Potassium 964mg, Carbohydrates 12g, Fiber 3g, 2gSugars, Proteins 23g

WEDNESDAY

Breakfast

Gingerbread Breakfast Quinoa Bake with Banana

A perfect one for that chilled morning.

Prep Time of 10 minutes, Cook Time of 80 minutes and a total time 90 minutes

Servings—8

Ingredients

- Molasses (a quarter cup)
- Cinnamon (a tablespoon)
- Maple syrup (pure and a quarter cup)

- Ginger (a teaspoon and ground)
- 1 teaspoon ground cloves
- 2 teaspoon sraw vanilla extract
- Allspice(a half a teaspoon and ground)
- 1 cup quinoa uncooked
- Medium over-ripe one Bananas mashed (3 cups) (under 370g)
- 1/2 teaspoon salt
- Unsweetened almond milk (vanilla)(2½ cups)
- Slivered almonds (1/4 cups)

Instructions

1. In a two and a half—three dishes (quart baking dish), have it stirred in your banana (pressed), molasses, the syrup, ginger, cinnamon, some vanilla extract and cloves, all the spices including the salt until it's mixed properly. Put the quinoa in and stir properly until it's distributed evenly inside your banana mixture.
2. Whisk your milk (almond) to mix properly. Cover it and have it refrigerate overnight.
3. At dawn, heat up your oven (350 degrees) then whisk your mixture (quinoa)and ensure it has settled at the bottom.
4. Cover your pan using tinfoil then bake it till the liquid has been absorbed and your quinoa is set at the top. Takes about 60 minutes to 75 minutes.
5. Have your oven at high broil; sprinkle your almonds (sliced) in the pan, then gently depress in (your quinoa). Broil the almonds until they turn brown, in two to four minutes. Be vigilant they burn quite quickly
6. Give 10 minutes to cool.

Nutrition

Calories 21.3g, total fat 4.1g, sodium 211mg, potassium of 550mg,fibers of 4.0g, sugar 17.8g, proteins 4.5g

Lunch

Heirloom Tomato Toast

A healthy afternoon with no doubt.

1 serving

Ingredients

- Heirloom tomato, (one small and diced)
- Persian cucumber, (one and diced)
- One teaspoon olive oil (extra virgin)
- Oregano (a pinch and dried)
- Salt (kosher) and black pepper (ground freshly)
- whipped cream cheese (low-fat)(2 teaspoons)
- 2 pieces Trader Joe's Whole Grain Crispbread
- 1 teaspoon balsamic glaze

Instructions

1. In a bowl (medium), put in the tomato, the cucumber, some oil with the oregano; season using the salt as well as pepper.
2. Smear the bread with cream cheese and top with the mixture(tomato-cucumber) and balsamic glaze.

Nutrition

177 calories,24g carbs,3g protein,4g sugars, 8g fat

Dinner

Tempeh Tostadas (Smoky) with Cabbage Slaw (Mango)

My nutritionist always has this every evening, no wonder!

Prep Time of 10 minutes, Cooking Time of 15 minutes and a total time of 25 minutes

<u>Components</u>

- Tempeh (one 8-ounce cut in thin pieces and packaged)
- ½ teaspoon ground cumin
- ¼ cup soy sauce or liquid aminos
- 1 teaspoon chili powder
- Hot sauce(½-1 teaspoon) (quantity is optional)
- Liquid smoke (1/2 teaspoon)
- 6 corn tortillas
- Garlic (a half teaspoon powder)

- Onion (1/2 teaspoon powder)
- Black pepper (a half teaspoon)
- 1 teaspoon agave nectar
- red cabbage,(1½ cups and shredded)
- Mango (3/4 cup and diced)
- Cilantro (1/2 cup and minced and additional for topping)
- lime juice (1 tablespoon and fresh)
- Oil for cooking
- vinegar (apple cider, 1 teaspoon)
- Salt (¼ teaspoon)

Additional toppings: some lettuce, cilantro, salsa, avocado

Instructions

1. Oven heat at 350°F.
2. Put in the tempeh into a bowl (medium sized).
3. Put soy sauce into another bowl (small), chili powder, some hot sauce, the cumin, liquid smoke, some garlic and onion powder, and the pepper. Whisk properly. Pour the tempeh and stir properly until it is coated evenly. Put aside for about 5-10 minutes.
4. Place corn tortillas onto your baking pan. Lightly apply oil. Bake for 10 minutes till crispy and brownish.
5. In a skillet with moderate heat (medium), put in the tempeh. Let it cook in four to five minutes until it becomes slightly ready. Flip the tempeh and cook it fortime (three-four minutes).
6. As your tempeh and tortillas are cooking, put in the red cabbage, the mango, the cilantro, some lime juice, some vinegar, the agave, and finally the salt to a bowl (medium). Combine properly by stirring.

7. Put in the tempeh in the tortillas, topped with slaw and any other desired toppings.

THURSDAY

Breakfast

Greek Goddess Bowl

Prepare this in the morning, and you'll never be late for work.

Preparation Time 7 minutes, Cooking Time of 23 minutes for a total time of 30 minutes

Components

Chickpeas

- Sea salt (a quarter teaspoon)
- A tablespoon oil (coconut or avocado are best however omit if avoiding oil)
- 1 15-ounce can chickpeas
- Shawarma(spice blend 1 tablespoon) (or spices similar you have at hand)

- Maple syrup or coconut sugar(1 tablespoon)

Bowl

- Red pepper (1 batch) Hemp Tabbouleh (or parsley sub-chopped)
- ¾ cup vegan tzatziki
- ½ cup cherry tomatoes (halved)
- 1 medium carrot
- ½ cup green or kalamata olives
- 1 medium cucumber (sliced)

Instructions

1. Heat your oven (375 degrees) and have your baking pan ready.
2. Add the washed chickpeas mixing in a bowl with oil, salt, maple syrup, and Shawarma Spice Blend.
3. Add the seasoned chickpeas to your baking pan. Bake it for about 20-23 minutes till they(chickpeas) become a bit crispy and brown (golden).
4. Assemble the bowl dividing the tzatziki, olives tabbouleh (or parsley), cucumber, tomatoes, carrots (optional) between two (serving) bowls. Top with the cooked chickpeas then garnish with lemon juice.
5. Best when fresh, but you can separately store leftovers for 3-4 days in the fridge. Have the leftovers(chickpeas) in a container sealed and in moderate temperature.

Nutrition

Calories 519,fiber 13.3g, protein 12g, carbohydrates49.8,fat 34.5g, sugar 19.4g,saturated fat 20.7g, sodium 609mg

Lunch

Mini Chicken Shawarma

How much more heavenly can this chicken get!

8 servings

<u>Ingredients</u>

- Cumin (one teaspoon and ground)
- 1 lemon (juice as well as zest)
- ½ teaspoon smoked paprika
- ¼ cup olive oil—extra virgin
- 1 pound chicken tenders
- Black pepper (one teaspoon and freshly ground)
- ¾ teaspoon ground coriander
- 2 teaspoons garlic powder

Sauce

- 1¼ cups Greek yogurt
- Parsley (a quarter cup and freshly chopped)
- One tablespoon lemon juice
- 2 chopped tomatoes

- 1 garlic clove, grated
- 4 leaves romaine lettuce, have them shredded
- Salt (kosher) and black pepper (ground freshly)
- Red onions, (a half and thinly sliced)
- 2 tablespoons chopped fresh dill
- 1 grated garlic clove
- ½ English cucumber, thinly sliced
- 16 mini pita bread

Instructions

1. Making the Chicken—Put the chicken in a large sealable plastic bag. Mix the oil, paprika, lemon juice and zest, cumin, garlic powder, coriander as well as pepper combining into a bowl. Put the marinade in your bag, seal then toss the chicken well to coat. Allow your chicken to marinate in 30 minutes to 60 minutes time.
2. Making the Sauce—as the chicken marinates, stir your Greek yogurt together with garlic andjuice (lemon) and add in your parsley as well as dill seasoning it using some pepper and salt. Refrigerate after covering.
3. Heat a skillet (large) over moderate heat. Take out the chicken after marinating, letting the extra drip off, and cook until it's fully ready and becomes brownishon each side (about 4 minutes every side). Chop it as preferred.
4. For assembling, divide the chicken, lettuce, onion, cucumber and tomato evenly among the pitas.

Nutrition

4sugars, 13g proteins, 10g carbs,9g protein,0g sugars

Sauce

300 calories, 0g sugars, 5g fat,56g carbs, 216 calories, 16g fat

Dinner

Chickpea Vegetable Coconut Curry

All you need is some whole grain for some dipping.

4 servings

<u>Ingredient</u>

- 1 lime (halved)
- Red onion, (one and thinly sliced)
- Ginger,(one fresh tablespoon and minced)
- Garlic, (three cloves and minced)
- Red bell pepper, (one and thinly sliced)
- Two teaspoons of chili powder
- 3 tablespoons red curry paste

- One 14-ounce can coconut milk
- 1 small cauliflower (head), (in bite-sized florets)
- Coriander (one teaspoon and ground)
- 3 tbsp. red curry paste
- Extra virgin olive oil (1 teaspoon)
- 1½ cups frozen peas
- One 28-ounce can cooked chickpeas
- Cilantro (a fresh quarter cup and chopped)
- Black pepper and salt (freshly grounded)
- Steamed rice, for serving (optional)
- 4 scallions, thinly sliced

Directions

1. Heat your (olive) oil in moderate heat inside a bowl. Put in onion, bell pepper then sauté until it's nearly tender for about 4-5 minutes. Then put in the sauté, ginger and some garlic until fragrant for about a minute.
2. Put in the cauliflower and combine well by tossing. Stir your coriander in with chile, red curry then cook until the mixture slightly darkens for a minute.
3. Stir in the coconut milk then bring your mixture to simmer over medium-low temperature. Cover the pot and continue simmering until your cauliflower is tender, 8 to 10 minutes.
4. With the lid off have the lime juice squeezed to curry form combining well by stirring. Put your chickpeas as well as peas in then season it using pepper and the salt, and smolder the mixture.
5. If desired serve it with rice and garnish every portion with cilantro (a tablespoon) and scallions (a tablespoon).

Nutrition

665 calories, 31g fats, 80g carbs, 26g protein,17g sugars

FRIDAY

Breakfast

Red Pepper, Feta Frittata and Kale

Preparation Time of five minutes, Cooking Time of thirty minutes and full time of thirty-five minutes

6-8 servings

Components

- Kale (two cups and chop)
- Feta cheese (half cup and crumbled)
- Oil spray
- Garlic (three cloves and minced)
- Black pepper (a quarter freshly cracked)
- Sea salt (a quarter teaspoon)
- Red pepper-bell (one medium and in dices)
- Eggs (eight large)
- Skim milk (half a cup)

Procedure

1. Have your oven heated at 350°. Spray a generous amount of oil.
2. Spread garlic, red peppers as well as the kale all in the dish (pie-dish). Sprinkle the feta on the vegetables.
3. Whisk your milk, eggs, pepper as well as salt in your container. Pour your mixture on the kale and the feta in the dish.
4. Get it baked in twenty-five to thirty-five minutes. Take them out of your oven then serve, instead, you could cool it before putting in the fridge and cover (must).

Lunch

Eggplant and Herb Flatbread.

You can now devour with powers invested by me!

Ingredients

For the Tahini Eggplant Dip

- 2 lbs eggplants
- 6 cloves garlic
- Cumin (a quarter teaspoon and grounded)
- Paprika2 (a quarter teaspoon)
- Olive oil
- A tablespoon of lemon juice
- A quarter cup of Tahini
- Salt (kosher) for taste

For the Flatbread

- Pizza dough (1/2 lb.)
- Scallions,(1 bunch and sliced—on a hard angle
- Mint (1 large handful), parsley and some basil leaves
- A tablespoon of lemon juice
- Salt (kosher) with pepper (black) (freshly cracked—for taste)
- Oil (olive)
- Feta (a half cup, crumbled)

Instructions

1. Using your fork, prick all over the eggplant. Have them roasted in the grill till every section is soft and blackened. Put the eggplant into your bowl and have it covered with a wrap (plastic). Put aside for cooling in 45 mins.
2. Chop inside of the peeled eggplant with the skin discarded and put in a clean bowl (large).
3. Mince the garlic (finely), putting in salt pinches while you combine by mincing. Add to the eggplant. Put in the cumin, oil, paprika, and some lemon juice with the eggplant and combine by stirring. Put in the tahini and combine by stirring. Taste then regulate salt and the lemon juice as preferred.
4. Have the oven at 450 degrees.
5. Using little flour on your surface, roll the dough (thin) into a rectangular size like that of a sheet pan. Move the dough to an oiled baking sheet drizzle with oil (olive). Baking takes place for 8-12 mins till it turns to a gold color. Take out of the oven then slather using the eggplant (mixture).

6. In a bowl (small), mix the scallions, basil, mint and parsley and toss using salt, pepper and lemon juice. Drizzle using oil (olive) and then toss. Put in the herb mixture on the eggplant layer and finish with the feta. Serve immediately.

Dinner

Chickpea Vegetable Coconut Curry

Find something to deep in, break, a muffin perhaps?

Preparation 10 minutes, Cooking 20 minutes and a total of 30 minutes

Servings—4

Ingredients

- 1 red bell pepper, sliced thinly
- Ginger, (a tablespoon fresh and minced)
- One red onion, sliced thinly
- olive oil(one tablespoon—extra virgin)
- Chile powder (two teaspoons)
- 3 minced garlic cloves
- Cauliflower(head),(one small and in bite-sized florets)
- One teaspoon ground coriander
- Three tablespoons red curry paste
- One 14-ounce can coconut milk
- 1 lime, halved
- 1½ cups frozen peas
- Steamed rice, for serving (optional)
- ¼ cup chopped fresh cilantro
- One 28-ounce can cooked chickpeas
- Black pepper(ground freshly) and salt
- Scallions, (4, and sliced thinly)

Directions

1. Have the oil heated (olive) inside a pot (big) with moderate heat. Put in your onion as well as bell pepper,

and then sauté till tender for 4 to 5 minutes. Put in your garlic with ginger then quickly frytill they are sweet-scented for 1 minute.

2. Put in the cauliflower then toss well for the combination. For your mixture to slightly darken, have your red curry, Chile powder and coriander stirred in then cook.

3. Stir in the coconut milk then have the mixture simmer in medium-low temperatures. Have the pot covered then continue simmering until your cauliflower is tender, 8 to 10 minutes.

4. Squeeze the lime juice in the curry, combine by stirring well. Put in the chickpeas as well as peas, with some salt and pepper season it, and have the mixture simmer.

5. Serve with rice, if desired. Have every portion garnished using one tablespoon of scallions as well a tablespoon of cilantro.

Nutrition

665 calories,31g fat,80g carbs, 26g protein,17g sugars

SATURDAY

Breakfast

Feta Frozen Yogurt

The richness of flavor and nutrients.

Ingredients

- Yoghurt
- Feta
- Honey

Instructions

Yogurt (frozen) to be precise. You'll basically blend your honey, yogurt, and feta, then have it in a pan then freeze. Once it's frozen, have it in chunks then blitz in a blender, additional bits of water or some milk to fasten things, till you get some creamy sweet-yet-tangy yogurt!

Nutrition

10g fats, 161 calories, 7g carbs, sodium 329mg, 12g sugar, 0g fiber, 7g protein

Lunch

Pesto Quinoa Bowls with Roasted Veggies and Labneh

Get your groove on, we're grilling something.

4 servings

<u>Ingredients</u>

- 1 medium zucchini, cubed
- Cherry tomatoes, (a pint and sliced into halves)
- Olive oil—extra virgin
- 1 large Japanese eggplant (cubed)
- 1 cup quinoa, rinsed
- 1 cup of labneh or Greek yogurt
- A handful of cilantro or parsley (or both), roughly chopped
- A handful of romano (or green) beans
- Salt(kosher) and black pepper(ground freshly)

- Pesto (half a cup) (either bought or homemade)
- 1 garlic clove, minced
- Juice from ½ lemon

Instructions

1. Have the oven heated till 400 degrees align your baking pan (a large on)using some paper and position the eggplant, beans, zucchini, and cherry tomatoes on it. Drizzle with some oil (olive) on the veggies and season using some salt and pepper. For thirty to forty minutes, roast your veggies till caramelized and soft.
2. Meanwhile, put in the quinoa in a medium saucepan along with water (two cups)and your pinch of salt. Boil, cover, then simmer and cook for about 15 minutes. When the quinoa has cooked, fluff using a fork, then allow it to cool. Once the quinoa has cooled slightly, toss with the pesto.
3. Mix the labneh, garlic, herbs, and lemon juice together into a bowl.
4. By adding your quinoa, assemble every bowl and have your veggies resemble a rainbow by arranging in rows. Then have your dollop of labneh beside it.

Nutrition

862 calories,42g fat,96g carbs,32gprotein,23g sugars

Dinner

Roasted Brussels Sprouts Quinoa

One colorful and easy recipe

Preparation Time of ten minutes, Cooking Time of twenty minutes and full time of thirty minutes

Ingredients

- Red onion (one large and sliced)
- Olive oil—extra virgin (two tablespoons)
- Carrots (six large, peeled and in edible sizes)
- Brussels sprouts (one pound), halved
- Quinoa (one cup and rinsed)
- Thyme (two teaspoon and fresh)
- Pepper (grounded freshly) and salt (kosher)
- Chicken stock (two cups)

Instructions

1. Have your oven heated at 450°. On your baking pepper, get the carrots tossed, onions, Brussels sprouts with the oil; get them seasoned with pepper and salt.
2. Have your veggies roasted till fork-tender in fifteen to twenty minutes.
3. Using your microwave-safe container, get your chicken stock combined with quinoa as well as thyme; have them seasoned using pepper and salt. Use wraps (plastic to cover your container then microwave at high for 6 minutes. If there's a lot of liquid remaining, microwave until it's absorbed, for an addition of three minutes.

4. Move your veggies as well as any remaining olive oil from the baking sheet to the container and combine by stirring; using pepper and salt have it seasoned.

Nutrition

11g fat, 56g carbs, 371 calories,14g protein, 11g sugars

WEEK 2 DIET PLAN

SUNDAY

Breakfast

Greek Omelette Casserole

The only way to start your day feeling like royalty.

Preparation Time of 10 minutes, Cooking Time of 35 minutes and a total time of 45 minutes

Ingredients

- Spinach(8 ounces and fresh)
- Eggs(12)
- Garlic(two cloves and minced)
- Two cups of whole milk
- Artichoke salad(12-ounce jar) (with peppers and olives), chopped and drained

- Tomato (5-ounce sundried and crumbled) feta cheese
- Chopped dill(1 tablespoon fresh) (1 teaspoon of dried dill)
- A teaspoon of oregano and dried
- A teaspoon of lemon pepper
- A teaspoon of salt
- Olive oil,(4 teaspoons and divided)

Procedure

1. Have the oven heated till 375. Have your herbs and salad chopped(artichoke).
2. Ensure the skillet is in moderate heat then put 1 table spoon oil. Sauté up the spinach and the garlic until they are wilted for about 3 minutes.
3. Have your baking dish oiled properly before layering your salad and spinach evenly.
4. In the meantime, have eggs, milk, herbs, salt as well as the pepper (lemon) whisked together properly in a bowl.
5. On your vegetables have the mixture (egg) poured in then sprinkled using cheese(feta). Have it bake at the middle of your oven for approximately 35-40 mins to have it firm in the middle.

Nutrition

Calories196,Fiber1g, Fats 12g, Carbohydrates 5g, Sugars 3g, Sodium536mg, Protein10g

Lunch

Greek Yogurt Chicken Salad Stuffed Peppers

Finally something addictive yet healthy!

Preparation 30 min, Total: 30 min

6 servings

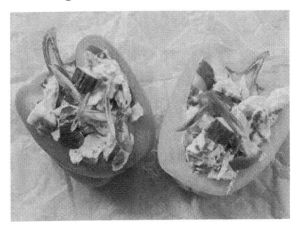

<u>*Ingredients*</u>

- ⅔ cup Greek yogurt
- Dijon mustard(two tablespoons)
- ½ cup of freshly chopped parsley
- Rice vinegar(two tablespoons and seasoned)
- Salt(kosher) and black pepper(ground freshly)
- Meat from 1 rotisserie chicken, cubed
- 4 stalks celery, sliced
- 3 bell peppers, halved and seeds removed
- 1 bunch scallions, sliced and divided
- 1-pint cherry tomatoes, quartered and divided
- ½ English cucumber, diced

Instructions

1. Inside a medium container, whisk your Greek yogurt together with mustard as well as rice vinegar; season it with some pepper and salt. Stir in your parsley.
2. Put in your celery, chicken and three quarters of each i.e. tomatoes, scallions, and cucumbers. For combining stir properly.
3. Divide the chicken salad on the bell pepper boats.
4. Garnish with the remaining cucumbers, scallions, and tomatoes.

Nutrition

10g sugar, 3g fat, 116 calories, 16g carbs,7g protein

Dinner

Sweet Potato Noodles with Almond Sauce

A new cuisine? Prepare for that sweet dream effect.

Preparation for 5 minutes, Cooking time for 15 minutes and a total time of 20 minutes

4 servings

<u>Components</u>

- All-purpose flour (three tablespoons)
- Olive oil-extra virgin (2 tablespoons)
- Shallots(three and minced)
- Garlic (2 cloves and minced)
- Almond sauce
- Unsweetened almond milk(2 cups plain)
- Two tablespoons of Dijon mustard
- Black pepper and salt (ground freshly)
- Sweet potato noodles
- Sweet potatoes, (3, cut into noodles using a spiralizer)
- Roughly torn kale(4 cups)
- Salted almonds (1/2 cup toasted and roughly toasted)

Instructions

1. Preparing the Almond dip: Have your oil heated inside a pot with moderate temperatures. Put in garlic as well as shallots then sauté until fragrant, for about a minute.
2. As you put in the flour and as it cooks stir constantly for a minute. Adding in your milk (almond), don't forget to whisk continuously to avoid the formation of lumps. Have it whisked in some moderate temperature till your mixture is simmered. Simmer for about four to five minutes.
3. Using pepper and salt season your sauce after you've whisked in your Dijon mustard. Have your sauce covered and warmed using low temperatures as you prepare your noodles.
4. Make the Sweet Potato Noodles: Have your oil heated in moderate temperatures inside a sauté casserole. Put in sweet potato noodles then sauté having them tossed from time to time to ensure they come out tender for approximately five to six minutes.
5. Put in your kale then toss it till it wilts. Have the sauce and toss added until the noodles are well coated.
6. Just before serving, add the almonds and combine them by tossing then have it seasoned using pepper and salt.

Nutrition

Almond Sauce

4g sugars, 139 calories, 3g proteins, 8g fat,14g carbs

Sweet Potato Noodles

5g sugars, 256 calories,25g carbs, 16g fat,6g protein

MONDAY

Breakfast

Veggie Egg Cups

A healthy one for that egg lover.

Preparation Time of five minutes, Cooking Time of twenty minutes and full time of twenty minutes

12 servings

Components

- Pepper (one red bell chopped and deseeded)
- Spinach sliced (1.5 cups 9 g)
- 100 ml (0.4 cups) milk
- 6 large eggs
- Brie cheese (75g chopped—2.7 oz)
- Salt

Procedure

1. Have your oven heated to350degrees then oil your 12-hole muffin tray.
2. Beat together the milk and eggs.
3. Mix all other ingredients.
4. Divide your combination (egg) equally into muffin cups then have them bake for about 18-20 minutes till ready.
5. Let the egg cups at least cool for about 5 minutes afterwards then remove it from the tray and enjoy while warm or wait and eat when cold.

Nutrition

Protein 4g, Fat 4g, Saturated Fat 1g, Calories 62kcal, Carbohydrates 1g, Cholesterol 88mg, Sodium 80mg, Potassium 113mg

Lunch

Mezze Plate with Toasted Za'atar Pita Bread

You'll thank me later, enjoy!

Preparation Time is 10 minutes, Cooking Time is 5 minutes bringing a total time of 15 minutes

Servings (four)

<u>Components</u>

- One cup hummus
- Four tablespoons olive oil (extra virgin)
- 4 teaspoons za'atar
- A cup of Greek yogurt
- Kosher salt and black pepper (ground freshly)
- Four wheat pita rounds (whole)
- 1 cup marinated artichoke hearts
- 1 cup sliced roasted red peppers

- 4 ounces salami
- 2 cups assorted olives
- 2 cups cherry tomatoes

Instructions

1. Heat up a skillet (large) over some moderate-high heat. Ensure you've brushed all both sides of every pita using oil (olive) then season it using the za'atar.
2. As you work in batches, put in the pita and have it toasted in your pan (skillet) till it becomes brown (golden),each 2 mins per side. Afterwards cut every pita to quarters.
3. Have the Greek yogurt seasoned with salt and pepper.
4. When assembling, divide the pitas, hummus Greek yogurt, artichoke hearts, olives, roasted red peppers, salami, and tomatoes among four plates.

Nutrition

731 calories, 8g sugars, 48g fat, 26g proteins,62g carbs

Dinner

Greek Lemon Chicken Soup

The Greek goddess of sweetness at work!

Preparation Time of 10 mins, Cooking Time of 20 mins ringing a total time of 30 minutes

8 servings

Components

- One sweet onion
- Olive oil (three tablespoons)
- 8 cloves garlic, minced
- 10 cups chicken broth
- Lemon, one large and zested
- Chicken breasts skinless and boneless(two)
- Couscous(one cup pearl and Israeli)
- red pepper(a half teaspoon and mashed)
- feta(2 ounces and fragmented)
- chive(1/3 cup and chopped)
- Pepper and salt

Instructions

1. Put in oil (olive) inside your sauce pot (six to eight quart) with moderate-low temperatures. Have the onion peeled and quartered then slice it to strips (thin). Sauté your minced garlic with onion once your oil becomes hot for about 3-4 minutes for it to soften.
2. Put in your broth (chicken), your chicken breasts as well as red pepper (crushed) and lemon zest inside your pot.

To make it boil, raise your heat and make sure it is covered. Once it has started boiling, have your heat down to moderate levels (medium) so as to simmer for the next five minutes.

3. With one teaspoon of salt as well as black pepper, have your couscous stirred in to taste. Have it Simmer in at five minutes then turn off the heat.

4. With tongs, pull the chicken breasts out of your pot. Using any fork as well as tongs get the chicken shredded. Return it back to the pot. In the meantime, have the crumbled feta cheese with chopped up chive stirred in. For better tasting add pepper and salt as preferred. Enjoy it while served warm.

Nutrition

Calories 286, Fat 11g, 2g fat (Saturated), 32mg Cholesterol, Potassium 613mg, Carbs 31g, Fibers 2g, Sugar 3g

TUESDAY

Breakfast

Cauliflower Fritters with Hummus

Terrific Tuesday with some cauliflowers!

Preparation Time—20 mins. Cook Time—1 h

4 servings

Ingredients

- Olive oil(two and a half tablespoon), separated, additional for frying
- Onion(one cup a half onion and chopped)
- Garlic(two tablespoon and minced)
- Two 15-ounce can chickpeas, divided
- Diced green onion, for garnish
- ½ teaspoon salt

- Cauliflower(two cups a half large head in small pieces)
- Black pepper
- Hummus, of choice, for topping

Instructions

1. Have your oven heated at 400°.
2. Take the chickpeas (drained and rinsed) then put in a dishtowel, for proper drying. Afterwards, have the chickpeas into a bowl (large) without losing skins then have it tossed with a tablespoon of oil. Have them spread into a pan avoiding overcrowding them, afterwards sprinkle pepper and salt on them.
3. For twenty minutes, have the chickpeas baked, ensure to stir properly and keep baking for five to ten minutes more till crispy.
4. After your chickpeas, have been roasted properly get them transferred onto your food mixer then process it till it breaks down as well as fragmented in nature. Avoid turning to flour to preserve texture. Put in a bowl then place aside.
5. Have the remnant oil (one and a half tablespoon) heated in a pan using moderate temperatures (medium). Put your onions with garlic then have it cooked till a bit brown (golden), for approximately two minutes. Put your cauliflower (chopped) then have them cooked for two more minutes, till it turns brownish.
6. Turn your heat low then have your pan covered. Let your cauliflower cook till they become tender and onions golden and also in caramel form, keenly stirring. This takes approximately three to five minutes.
7. Move your mixture to the mixer. Have it drained up then the chickpeas rinsed and as well have it in the food

mixer, all with a pinch of pepper and salt. Have it blend till it's smooth, then as your mixture begins taking a ball form, stop to scrape the sides as needed.

8. After transferring your cauliflower mixture to a container as well as added a half a cup of chickpea crumbs (roasted), combine well by stirring.

9. With just needed oil, lightly have the bottom of your pan covered and heated in moderate temperatures. For approximately two to three minutes, have your patties cooked till brown (golden),flipping then cooking once more.

Nutrition

14g proteins, 9g sugars, calories 333, fat 13g, 45g carbs, sodium 323mg, fiber 13g

Lunch

Salmon Bowl Up with Farro, Black Beans with Tahini Dressing

Make your belly smile!!

Preparation for 10 minutes, cooking for 30 minutes bringing a total time of 40 minutes

1 serving

Components

- Olive oil (extra virgin)(6 tablespoons divided)
- Zest and juice of 1 lemon
- Turmeric,(a half teaspoon divided)
- Garlic (a quarter teaspoon powder)
- Tahini (2tablespoons)
- Salt (kosher) and freshly ground black pepper
- Farro (¼ cup)
- Black beans (a half cup and cooked)
- Cumin(a half teaspoon)

- Salmon(6ounces)
- Paprika (one and a half teaspoon and smoked)
- Coriander (a half teaspoon of coriander)
- Lettuce leaves (4 boston)
- Avocado, (1/2 thinly sliced)
- Scallions, (2 thinly sliced)
- Fresno chile, (1/4 thinly sliced)

Instructions

1. In your bowl, whisk the tahini, the zest (lemon), the juice (lemon), the ¼ teaspoon of the turmeric as well as the garlic powder. Gradually put in 3 tablespoons of the oil(olive) and then whisk till the dressing is thick and is well emulsified. Have it seasoned using pepper and salt.
2. Bring your farro and a cup of water to simmer in a pot (small) with moderate temperatures (medium). Simmer in low temperature still your farro becomes relatively very tender, approximately 20 to 25 minutes. Place it aside.
3. Combine beans, oil (olive)(a tablespoon) and also your cumin in a bowl(small). Put aside.
4. Seasonup the salmon with smoked paprika, remaining turmeric (1/4 teaspoon), coriander pepper as well as salt. Have your remnant oil (2 tablespoons olive) heated into a pan (non-stick) with moderate temperatures. Put in your salmon and then cook, till it browns on one side and opaque at the center, for about 5 minutes.
5. Put the lettuce leaves at the base of the serving bowl. Top it with farro, the black beans and the salmon. Garnish it with the avocado, the scallions and also the sliced chile; drizzle up with the dressing.

Nutrition

1,732 calories, 7g sugars, 137g fat, 59g protein, 81g carbs

Dinner

Jerk Shrimp with Pineapple Rice

That enticing perfect blend?

Ingredients

For the Rice

- Butter (1 tablespoon)
- Pineapple juice (half a cup)
- Pineapple chunks (one cup and drained)
- Water (one cup)
- Crushed red pepper (a quarter teaspoon and crushed)
- Spice powder-curry (a teaspoon)
- Garlic (a half teaspoon powder)
- Onion (a half teaspoon powdered)
- Salt (half teaspoon)
- Molasses (1 tablespoon pure)
- Citrus juice, (1 tablespoon and squeezed freshly)
- Rice-basmati (one cup)
- Cilantro,(2-4 tablespoons and chopped)

For the Shrimp

- Garlic,(2 cloves and minced
- Butter(2 tablespoons)
- Shrimp(4cups and small)
- Caribbean seasoning-jerk (two and a quarter teaspoons)

- Onion—green (chopped)

Instructions

Rice

1. Put water in a pot, together with pineapple juice and chunks, red pepper, butter, garlic and curry powder, citrus juice, onion powder, glucose, and salt. Let it boil then stir in the rice, and let it boil in moderate temperatures.
2. Cover after simmering in low temperatures. For twenty minutes, cook your rice till soft and all the water absorbed.
3. Take out of the heat source and allow the rice to stay covered for ten minutes. Fluff up the rice using a fork then have the cilantro stirred in.

Shrimp

1. Have your butter melted inside a pan with moderate temperatures. With your garlic stirred in, let it cook for one to two minutes. (Careful with the garlic not to burn it).
2. Reduce the heat; get the shrimp stirred in as well as the jerk dressing. Have the shrimp cooked for two to three minutes till ready.
3. With the heat off, get your shrimp tossed with your preferred amount of green onions. Have it served with rice.

WEDNESDAY

Breakfast

Mediterranean Tuna Salad

One to keep you full for hours!

Prep Time of eight minutes and full time of eight minutes

Two servings

Components

- Wild selections solid white albacore tuna(1 in can and water drained)
- Olive oil(2 tablespoons)
- Olives(8 kalamata in slices)
- Red peppers (a quarter cup roasted and in dices)
- Lemon juice (1 tablespoon)
- Capers(2tablespoons)
- Flat-leaf parsley optional (one tablespoon fresh and chopped)
- Pepper and salt for taste

Instructions

1. Put all the ingredients inside your bowl, after flaking apart the tuna using a fork mix them together.
2. You may put your leftovers in a fridge or serve the meal immediately.

Nutrition

21g protein, 250 calories, fibers 1g,fat17g,carbs 3g, 606mg sodium, 1g sugar

Lunch

Greek Lemon Chicken Skewers with Tzatziki Sauce

Bite, enjoy and flaunt your meal as you stroll around the house.

Preparation Time thirty minutes, Cooking Time of an hour and full time of one hour thirty minutes.

Six servings

Ingredients

Tzatziki Sauce

- Cucumber—European (a half and in dices)
- Olive oil—extra virgin (one tablespoon)
- Citrus juice (two tablespoons)
- Garlic—powder (a pinch)
- Greek yogurt(one cup)
- Black pepper(ground freshly) and salt
- ¼ cup fresh chopped dill

Skewers

- ¼ cup Greek yogurt
- 1 teaspoon dried oregano
- Pinch of cayenne pepper
- One lemon(juice and zest)
- One teaspoon garlic powder
- Chicken breast (one and a half pounds, skinless and boneless cut in a half inch strips)
- Black pepper (ground freshly) and salt
- Olive oil-extra virgin
- Parsley (a quarter mug and chopped)

Instructions

1. Make the Tzatziki: using a bowl put together the yoghurt, lemon juice, garlic powder, cucumber as well as oil for the combination. Have it seasoned with pepper and salt for tasting then get your dill stirred in.
2. Make the Skewers: Whisk in a bowl the lemon juice, yogurt, lemon zest, garlic powder, cayenne and oregano.
3. On the other hand, have your chicken in a different bowl and rubbed with the yoghurt and lemon mixture for proper coating
4. Let every skewer to have a chicken piece, weaving the strip back and forth as you thread it onto the skewer to secure it.
5. Using oil, get your skewers brushed on each side then have it seasoned with pepper and salt. As you work in batches, cook in a grill pan till its charred nicely on each side for four to five minutes on each side.
6. Have it garnished using parsley as well astzatziki sauce on the side then serve.

Nutrition

Tzatziki Sauce

2g sugars, 5g fat, 68 calories, 4g proteins, 3g carbs

Skewers

170 calories, 2g carbs, 27gfat, 6g protein, 1g sugars

Dinner

Five-Ingredient Lemon Chicken Asparagus

Ready to rejuvenate up your tummy with this meal?

Prep Time of ten minutes, Cooking Time of ten minutes

4 servings

Components

- Flour (a quarter cup)
- Chicken breasts(one lb. and boneless and skinless)
- Butter(2 tablespoons)
- Asparagus(1-2 cups and chopped)
- Honey (2 tablespoons) and butter (two tablespoons)
- Salt (a half teaspoon) and dab for taste
- Lemon pepper seasoning(1 teaspoon)
- Lemons, (2 and sliced)
- Some parsley for topping (not a must)

Instructions

1. **Chicken**: Have your chicken breast wrapped in a plastic wrap and pound until each piece is three quarter an inch in thickness. With the pepper ,salt, and flour inside your dish, gently have every chicken coated by tossing in. Get the butter melted in a skillet with moderate to high temperatures; put in your poultry then sauté in three to five minutes for every part, till it becomes brown, having sprinkled every part using lemon pepper inside your pan. Once it's properly cooked as well as browned put on a plate.
2. **Asparagus veggies and citrus/lemon**: Have the chopped asparagus into your pan. In a few minutes, let it sautétill light green having a soft crisp. Take out of your

pan and place separately. With your lemon(slices) flatly placed at the bottom in few minutes, have it cooked on each part without stirring to allow them to caramelize and allow brown pieces from the poultry left inside your pan from butter and chicken. Take the lemons out of your pan and put separately.

3. **Assembling**: Lay the ingredients back to your skillet; asparagus, the poultry as well as the lemon (slices) at the top.

Nutrition

Cholesterol 98mg, Sodium 343.9mg, Total Carbohydrate 16.1g,Total Fat 9g,Sugars 9.4g, Protein 27.4g, Vitamin A 71.7µg, Vitamin C 3.8mg

THURSDAY

Breakfast

Spinach & Tomato Goat Cheese Quiche

One to leave you all full and sate with appetizing memories!

6 servings

Ingredients

- 1 cup egg whites
- 2 ounces goat cheese
- Onion (a half and chopped)
- Garlic (one clove and minced)
- One teaspoon avocado oil sub-EVOO if needed
- 4 cups of fresh spinach
- 4 eggs
- 1 Roma Tomato cut into slices
- Pepper and salt

Procedure

1. Have your oven heated at 375F.
2. Sauté chopped onion together with garlic (if using fresh) in one to two minutes until tender.
3. Put in your spinach stirring it till wilted, remove from heat.

4. In a bowl (medium), whisk eggs, the egg whites, the garlic powder (if you never use fresh), pepper and salt. Put your spinach combination in and then properly mix.
5. Pour into an 8×8 dish or 8-inch cake pan, spread out ingredients evenly.
6. Put in crumbled goat cheese evenly and top with tomato slices.
7. Bake till your eggs become firm. Allow it to cool five to ten minutes to serving.

Nutrition

Calories 104, fat 45, fat (saturated) 2g, 113mg cholesterol, 166mg sodium, 189mg potassium, carbs 3g, 10g proteins

Lunch

Eggplant Pizza

Low-carb, gluten-free and all quick to prepare

Preparation Time for fifteen minutes, a Cooking Time of twenty minutes and full time of thirty five minutes.

Six servings

Ingredients

- Eggplants(1 large)
- Mozzarella cheese(1½ cups and shredded)
- Oil—olive (a third cups)
- Black pepper (ground freshly) and salt
- Marinara sauce (1¼ cups) (bought or homemade)
- Cherry tomatoes,(2 cups and halved)
- Torn basil leaves(1/2 cup)

Instructions

1. Have the oven heated at 400°F.Get your baking paper lined up using a vellum paper.
2. Shred off all ends of the eggplant(s) off then cut into thick slices. Arrange up these slices on the baking sheets

and then brush all two sides on each slice using oil (olive). With pepper and salt season it.

3. Get your eggplant slices roasted till nearly tender, about ten to twelve minutes.

4. Take your trays out of the oven then spread about 2 tablespoons of marinara sauce on every piece. Top it generously with the mozzarella and then arrange about 3 to 5 cherry tomato pieces on each.

5. Return the pizzas back inside your oven then roast till you melt all cheese as well as have the tomatoes are now blistered, about 5 to 7 minutes more.

6. Serve the pizzas while hot and garnished with basil.

Nutrition

257 calories, 8g protein, 8g sugars, 20g fat, 13g carbs

Dinner

Baked Ginger Salmon(Sesame) in Parchment

That ginger essence all around your kitchen

Preparation Time of ten minutes, Cooking Time of twenty minutes bringing a fulltime of thirty minutes.

Four servings

Ingredients

- Zucchini (two, halved large and sliced thinly)
- Red onion,(one sliced thinly and halved)
- Lime,(one and quartered)
- 1 teaspoon sesame oil
- Garlic (one teaspoon powder)
- Honey (two tablespoons)
- Flakes—red pepper (a pinch)
- Four 6-ounce skinless salmon fillets
- Soy sauce (two tablespoons)
- Ginger (two tablespoons fresh and grated)
- Sesame seeds (four teaspoons)

Instructions

1. Have your oven heated at 350°F. Get parchment (four pieces) prepared (fifteen to seventeen inches). Make creases by folding every piece into a half then have it unfolded unfold and secluded.
2. Whisk your oil (sesame), ginger, soy sauce, honey, pepper flakes and garlic powder and combine inside a bowl.

3. Get the parchment packets built each at a go. Have a quarter zucchini placed on one parchment piece evenly layered then top with red onions (a quarter). Using the lime piece, squeeze on top of the veggies.
4. On the veggies put your salmon fillet. With soy sauce combination, generously brush it then have it topped using one teaspoon of sesame seeds.
5. Having the empty parchment side on your salmon, get your two edges inwardly folded to the salmon ensuring extra creases to seal your package fully.
6. Do the same with remaining ingredients as well as parchment. Take the ready packages to the baking paper then have them baked till your salmon is well cooked, approximately sixteen to twenty minutes.
7. Take the veggies and fish out of packets and move to plates to serve, or rather have slits on top of your parchments then have them served inside the paper.

Nutrition

14g sugars,26g fat, 21g carbs, 468 calories, 39g protein

FRIDAY

Breakfast

Chocolate Oats (overnight) with Chia Seeds & Warm Strawberry Vanilla Compote

Preparation Time of five minutes, Cooking Time of five minutes and a full time of ten minutes.

1 serving

Components

- Unsweetened organic soy milk (half a cup)
- Chia seeds (one tablespoon)
- Salt (an eighth teaspoon)
- Oats (a third a cup)
- 1 container {5.3 oz} Chocolate Coconut Yogurt
- Maple syrup (one teaspoon and pure)
- Salt (one pinch)
- Cacao Nibs (optional), for serving
- Strawberries (one cup fresh and frozen)
- Vanilla-extract (one teaspoon and pure)

Instructions

Making the Oats

1. Get a bowl and put the milk, yoghurt, oats, salt, chia seeds in. For your oats to soften, have them for three to four hours in a fridge or overnight. Having strawberries that are frozen, you can let them thaw overnight or use the microwave for defrosting.

Strawberry Vanilla

2. In moderate temperatures, get your skillet heated. With your strawberries already defrosted inside, have them sauté in one minute before mashing using your preferred fork or equipment. Afterwards, put in the vanilla as well as glucose and have them stirred as you cook in about one to two minutes.

Serving the meal

➢ Top up your overnight oats using strawberry vanilla, then if necessary drizzle at the top using cacao nibs the cacao.

Lunch

Cold Lemon Zoodles

When you need that quick fix!

Preparations 20 min, Total: 20 min

4 servings

Ingredients

- Garlic (a half teaspoon powder)
- Oil—olive(a third a cup)
- Lemon, (1zested, juiced)
- Dijon mustard(1/2 teaspoon)
- Zucchini, (3 medium cut up into noodles)
- Radishes, (1 bunch and thinly sliced)
- Black pepper and salt(ground freshly)
- Thyme (one tablespoon fresh and chopped)

Instructions

1. Whisk to combine the garlic, lemon juice, and zest and mustard in a container.
2. Whisk for the combination of the gradually added oil. Have it seasoned using pepper and salt.
3. Get your zucchini noodles tossed inside a container as well as your radishes. Put in your seasoning as you properly toss for proper coating.
4. Serve immediately, garnished with fresh thyme.

Nutrition

198 calories, 19g fat, 8g carbs, 2g protein, 5g sugars

Dinner

Vegan Avocado Caprese Pasta Salad

That serving dish will be empty in no time.

Preparation Time of ten minutes, Cooking Time of eight minutes and a full time of eighteen minutes

6 servings

<u>*Ingredients*</u>

- Citrus juice (1 tablespoon fresh)
- Maple syrup(1 teaspoon) or maybe agave nectar
- Oil—olive (two tablespoons)
- Garlic (three cloves, minced one tablespoon)
- Salt (½ teaspoon)
- Avocado, (1 and chopped)
- Balsamic vinegar (1/4 cups)
- Bag brown rice pasta(1 16-ounce)
- Cherry tomatoes,(1, 8-ounce pint and halved—one and a half cups)
- Basil, (one cup fresh and chop)
- Pepper (a quarter teaspoon)

Instructions

1. Have your pasta cooked as per the packaged instructions. Get them drained then put in a container.
2. Put tomatoes, the basil, and the avocado. Stir it until ingredients become evenly mixed.
3. Whisk the (olive) oil, balsamic vinegar, salt, garlic, lemon juice pepper, and maple syrup in a container then combine by stirring properly after you've poured in your pasta.

SATURDAY

Breakfast

Easy Baked Shakshuka with Fennel and Goat Cheese

Ingredients

- Garlic (2 cloves and crushed)
- Smoked paprika(1 teaspoon and smoked and ground)
- Olive oil—extra virgin (one tablespoon)
- Onion (a half medium and diced)
- Fennel(1 bulb and chopped)
- Goat cheese(2 ounces and crumbled or maybe sliced)
- Eggs(6 large)
- Rosemary (1tablespoon and chopped)
- Cumin (1½ teaspoon and ground)
- Tomatoes(128-ounce diced with no salt—canned)

Instructions

1. Heat up oven till 400 degrees.
2. Get your oil in the skillet heated over moderate temperatures. Sauté your onions then have them fennel cooked till it becomes tender, 5-7 minutes.
3. With your spices as well as garlic stirred in, have them cooked for an extra minute for aromatic purposes.
4. Put in the tomatoes then let it simmer. Cook till the liquid becomes thick, till 10 minutes. Crack open the eggs on the pan then distribute over the pan in an even manner.
5. Sprinkle up goat cheese with rosemary on. Transfer the dish slowly to your oven then in ten minutes, have it baked till all middle parts are set.

6. Top it with some fresh rosemary maybe or some other herbs.

Lunch

Greek Turkey Burgers with Tzatziki Sauce

Ever had a healthy burger?

Preparation Time of thirty-five minutes and fulltime of seventy minutes

Four servings

Ingredients

Turkey Burgers

- Egg(1)
- Parsley(1/2 cup and chopped and fresh)
- Bread crumbs(3/4 cups)
- Salt and black pepper (freshly ground)
- Dried oregano(1/2 teaspoon)
- Olive oil—extra virgin (one tablespoon)
- Onion (one sweet, minced)
- Garlic (two cloves and minced)
- Red pepper—flakes (a quarter teaspoon)
- Turkey (one pound and grounded)

Tzatziki Sauce

- Greek yogurt(1 cup)
- Lemon juice (two tablespoons)
- Garlic (one pinch powdered)
- Black pepper and salt (ground freshly)
- Parsley(a quarter cup fresh and chopped)

- Cucumber, (a half-European and diced)
- Extravirgin olive oil(1 tablespoon)

Burger Toppings

- Hamburger buns (4 whole wheat)
- Onion(1/2 red and sliced),
- Lettuce leaves(8 Boston)
- Tomatoes,(2 and sliced)

Instruction

1. Making the Burgers: Over a moderate temperature, get oil heated in your skillet. Put your onion in, then have it cooked till it is soft for three to four minutes. Get your garlic inside and then have it sautéed till aromatic for one more minute. Put aside to start cooling.
2. In a bowl (medium), mix up the cooled up onion mixture together with the egg, the parsley, the oregano, the redpepper flakes as well as ground turkey. Put in the bread crumbs, season them with some salt and the pepper, and mix well until combined.
3. Heat up the oven to 375°F. Form up the meat mixture to 4 patties of the same size. Get your skillet heated over moderate temperature then have it generously sprayed using the nonstick spray for cooking.
4. Put the burgers all up in a skillet then sear on every side till it is well brown, for four to five minutes on every part. Take the cooking pan inside your oven then cook till all burgers have been fully about 15-17 minutes more.
5. Making Tzatziki Sauce: To combine mix garlic powder, lemon juice, cucumber, and yoghurt inside a container.

Have it seasoned with pepper and salt stirring it to your parsley.

6. Making the Toppings: Put each burger at the bottom half-bun and top each with tzatziki (1/4 cup), with 2 lettuce leaves, the 2 tomato slices as well as top half in the bun.

Nutrition

Turkey Burger

326 calories, 22g carbs,fat 14g, sugars 6g, protein 27g

Tzatziki Sauce

102 calories, 7g fat, 5g carbs, 6g protein, 3g sugars

Burger Toppings

132 calories, 3g fat, 23g carbs, 5g protein, 5g sugars

Dinner

Pumpkin Pasta (Skillet) with Spinach and Mushrooms

Gratitude for the greens

Preparation Time of five minutes, Cooking Time of twenty-five minutes and a full time of thirty minutes

Four servings

Components

- Hokkaido pumpkin (a half to asmall medium-sized)
- Olive oil (2 teaspoons divided)
- Salt and black pepper
- 1 garlic
- Whole wheat pasta(350 grams)
- Mushrooms sliced (200 grams)
- Raw spinach(140 grams)
- Nutmeg (1/4 teaspoon)
- Walnuts (4 tablespoons)
- Pumpkin oil(4 teaspoons)
- 235 ml vegetable broth
- Dried basil 1 teaspoon
- Sage (½ teaspoon dried)

Instructions

1. Have your oven heated at 180°C.Get your pumpkin chopped to little pieces. Ensure your tray has been laid down using a vellum paper then drizzled using oil. Have your present pumpkin sprinkled using pepper and salt. Get your garlic top cut and on the tray. Get it baked inside your oven for twenty minutes.

2. Cook pasta with the instructions given on its package. Have your skillet with heated oil then get the mushrooms sautéed for three minutes in moderate temperatures. Get your spinach in then have it cooked till tender in four to five minutes.

3. When pumpkin gets roasted, move it into a blender with the roasted peeled garlic as well as pulse it until its smooth, putting in the vegetable broth. Put spices and the herbs, not forgetting the salt, pepper for tasting.

4. Have your mushrooms, pasta, pumpkin puree and mushrooms combined. Get your meal sprayed using pumpkin oil as well as sprinkle the walnuts on top.

Nutrition

Saturated Fat 1g, Sodium 280mg, Fiber 4g, Sugars 5g Protein 18g, Calories 518, Total Fat 14g, Potassium 1209mg, Total Carbohydrates 87g

WEEK 3 DIET PLAN

SUNDAY

Breakfast

Cantaloupe Breakfast Bowl

Preparation Time of ten minutes and a fulltime of ten minutes

Two servings

Ingredients
- Cantaloupe (one whole)
- Blueberries (one cup)
- ¼ cup pecans chopped
- 2 tablespoons hemp seeds
- 1½ cups cottage cheese

Instructions
1. Wash cantaloupe and pat dry. Slice into halves and remove the seeds.
2. Fill each cantaloupe half with ¾ cup cottage cheese, and then top each half off with a half cup blueberries, 2 tablespoons chopped pecans, and 1 tablespoon hemp seeds.

Nutrition

Potassium 284mg, Fiber 3g, Protein 26g, Fat 23g, Calories 380kcal, Carbohydrates 19g, Saturated Fat 4g, Cholesterol 28mg, Sodium 617mg, Sugar 12g

Lunch

Harissa Chickpea Stew with Eggplant and Millet

Preparation Time 35 minutes, Cooking 10 minutes bringing atotal of 45 minutes

2 servings

Components

- A cup millet
- 3 garlic cloves (minced)
- Kosher salt
- 1 diced onion
- 2 tablespoons of ghee (or any other neutral high-heat oil)
- 1 14ounce can pureed tomatoes
- 1 large Japanese eggplant
- 1 bunch cilantro for garnish

- Black pepper(ground freshly)
- Chickpeas (one canned 14-ounce and drained)
- 2 tablespoons harissa paste

Instructions

1. Fill 2 cups water in a saucepan then put in the millet with some very little salt. Boil, then allow it to simmer and cook for 25 minutes. Once the millet is ready, fluff and let it to cool.
2. Heat oil (1 tablespoon) into a deep skillet with heat (medium). Put in your eggplant seasoned with pepper and salt, let it cook until it's tender and has that golden brown color, add more oil to prevent the eggplant from sticking on the skillet, do so for about 10 minutes.
3. Put the oil (a tablespoon) in the skillet with onions then cook till golden brown and tender.
4. Cook the garlic for a few minutes (2), and then season it with some pepper as well as salt, put in the chickpeas, harissa, tomatoes. Put your egg plant in the skillet and let it simmer for 10-15 minutes.
5. Divide your millet between bowls (2) and top with your stew. Garnish the millet with some leaves of cilantro after you've topped with the stew and enjoy.

Nutrition

600 calories, 17g sugars, 15g fat, 20g protein, 100g carbs

Dinner

Cold Lemon Zoodles

That soothing sweet feeling in the throat when swallowing this one.

Preparation 20 minutes, Total 20 minutes

4 servings

Ingredients

- Garlic (a half teaspoon powdered)
- Olive oil(a third a cup)
- 1 lemon, zested and juiced
- Dijon mustard (a half teaspoon)
- Zucchini (three medium and into noodle size)
- Radishes (one bunch sliced thinly)
- Thyme (one tablespoon fresh and chopped)
- Black pepper(ground freshly) and salt

Instructions

1. Get your garlic powder, mustard, lemon juice, and zest combined by whisking in a container.
2. Have your oil gradually added and combined by whisking. Using pepper and salt season your mixture.
3. Toss your zucchini noodles together with radishes inside a container. For the veggies to be well coated, put in your seasoning as you properly toss.
4. Serve immediately, garnished with fresh thyme.

Nutrition

2g protein, 5g sugars,198 calories, 19g fat, 8g carbs

MONDAY

Breakfast

Wild Alaska Salmon and Smashed Cucumber Grain Bowls

Having a wild desire for a healthy meal?

Preparation Time of fifteen minutes, Cooking Time of forty minutes and a fulltime of fifty-five minutes

4 servings

<u>Components</u>

- Garlic (one clove and minced)
- (A third cup) and oil—extra virgin (two tablespoons)
- Faro (two cups)
- Lemons (two and juiced)
- Dijon mustard (two tablespoons)
- Cucumber (one European and into one-inch pieces)
- Rice vinegar (a quarter cup and seasoned)
- Dill (a quarter cup fresh and chop)
- Salmon fillets—Alaska sockeye (four6-ounces)
- Black pepper (ground freshly) and salt (kosher)
- Parsley (a quarter cup fresh and chopped)
- Mint (a quarter cup fresh and chop)

<u>Procedure</u>

1. Boil salted your water from a large pot. Inside your hot water, put in the farro and let it be cooked till soft for twenty-five to thirty minutes before draining.

2. Transfer the farro to a container. Put in your garlic, mustard, citrus juice and a third cup olive oil; have it seasoned using pepper and salt.
3. In a different container, roughly smash the cucumber chunks using a fork. Add the rice vinegar then combine by tossing. Season using pepper and salt then add the parsley, mint and dill.
4. Have two tablespoons of oil heated in a saucepan over moderate temperatures. Get it seasoned using pepper and salt. Put in your fillets in hot oil then cook to desired doneness, 8 to 10 minutes.
5. Have your farro placed in your four plates. Get one salmon fillet roughly broken up in every plate then topped using herbs and cucumbers.

Nutrition

43g fat, 841 calories, 49g protein, 69g carbs, 8g sugars

Dinner

Cilantro Lime Chicken with Avocado Salsa

A practical explanation of tantalizing!

Preparation Time of fifteen minutes, Cooking Time of twelve minutes and a full time of twenty-seven minutes

6 servings

Components

Cilantro Lime Chicken:

- 2 tablespoons olive oil
- ¼ cup fresh cilantro
- Chicken breast (1.5 pounds and boneless)
- Citrus juice (a quarter cup)
- Salt (half teaspoon)
- Cumin (a half teaspoon and grounded)

Avocado Salsa:

- Avocados (four and diced)
- Red pepper (half teaspoon) flakes
- Garlic (one clove and minced)
- Cilantro (a half cup fresh and in dices)
- Lime juice (three tablespoons)
- Vinegar-red wine (half tablespoon)
- Salt

Procedure

1. Put a quarter cup cilantro, a quarter teaspoon salt, ground cumin, olive oil and lime juice (a quarter cup) then whisk properly till mixed.

2. Put your marinade and chicken into a bag (zip-lock) and allow the poultry marinate for fifteen minutes.
3. Have your grill heated at 400 degrees. Put your poultry in your grill and let every side cook for four to six minutes till it's ready. Remove and place aside when done.
4. Avocado Salsa: Put in three tablespoon citrus juice, avocado, vinegar, garlic, salt and half cup cilantro and slowly mix by tossing.
5. Using your salsa, top the lime chicken (cilantro).

Nutrition

Sodium 227mg, Fat 29g, Calories 373, Sugar 1g, Carbohydrates 14g, Fiber 10g, Protein 15 g, Cholesterol 33 mg

TUESDAY

Breakfast

Cappuccino Muffins

Preparation Time of ten minutes, Cooking Time of twenty minutes, 12 servings

Components

- Brown sugar(a half cup)
- One egg
- Cream (half cup)
- Flour (two cups all-purpose)
- Baking soda (one tablespoon)
- Salt (one pinch)
- One cup strong espresso or very strong brewed coffee cold
- Powdered sugar to garnish

Procedure

1. Have your oven heated at 350 F.
2. Get the muffin pan brushed using butter.
3. Put in your flour, salt and baking powder inside a container then mix.
4. Hole up at the middle of the flour and add sugar.
5. Beat egg and cream with a hand mixer.
6. Add the egg/cream mixture. And the coffee into the flour. Beat well with the hand mixer.
7. Pour the muffin mix into the muffin pan.
8. Bake for 20 minutes. Poke using a knife to make sure it's cooked. If otherwise bake some more.

9. Allow the muffins to cool and then decorate with powdered sugar.

Lunch

Greek Chicken (roasted), Farro Salad, and Oven Fries

Finger licki ng!!

PreparationTime of fifteen minutes, Cooking Time of forty minutes and full time of fifty-five minutes

4 servings

Components

- Dill (one tablespoon fresh and chopped)
- Oregano (one tablespoon fresh and chopped)
- Pound boneless chicken breasts
- Olive oil—extra virgin (two tablespoons)
- Vinegar—balsamic (two tablespoon)
- One pound russet potatoes, (wedges)
- Tzatziki (yogurt), some olives, some cucumber, some red onion, just for serving
- Vinaigrette—red wine
- Vinegar—red wine (three tablespoons)
- Honey (one teaspoon)
- Red peppers,(one to two and sliced)
- Farro (two cups and cooked)
- Lemon (one and juiced)
- Oregano (one tablespoon fresh and chopped)
- Garlic (one to two cloves grated/minced)
- Red pepper (one pinch and crushed) flakes
- Pepper and salt (kosher)
- 1 tablespoon paprika
- Butter lettuce (one head torn roughly)

- 8 ounces feta, cubed

Instructions

1. Heat your oven up having 425 degrees F.
2. Combine your poultry on the rimmed baking paper to combine chicken, cooking fat/oil (1 tablespoon), balsamic vinegar, some dill, some oregano, some paprika, garlic as well as both pepper and salt (one large pinch). Toss well to evenly coat the chicken. Put in potatoes, bell pepper then have them tossed using the remaining 1 tablespoon oil with pepper and salt (pinch). Place everything to that even layer. Roast for 40-45 minutes, tossing it halfway through the cooking till the chicken has been properly cooked and potatoes are golden. After the chicken has cooled, have it shredded into pieces.
3. How assembly is done: do smear little tzatziki to the bottom of 4 bowls(for salad). Put in your farro, some lettuce, the bell peppers, the potatoes as well as the chicken. Sprinkle your feta topping as you desire using cucumber, olives, not forgetting the red onions. Drizzle up using your red wine (vinaigrette).

Red Wine Vinaigrette

1. Combine all the ingredients into a bowl or then whisk properly so as to combine. To confirm taste so as to regulate seasoning as you'd like.

Nutrition

Calories 782 kcal

Dinner

Mediterranean Baked Sweet Potatoes

Spoilt for choice on what to put in your mouth first?

Preparation Time of five minutes, Cooking Time of twenty-five minutes and a full time of thirty minutes

Four Serving

Components

- 4 medium (a third a pound each) sweet potatoes
- One 15-ounce can chickpeas
- 1/2 tablespoon olive oil
- Cumin (a half teaspoon), coriander (a half teaspoon), cinnamon (a half teaspoon),paprika
- Lemon juice or a pinch of salt

Garlic herb sauce

- Dill (three quarter to one teaspoon and dried)
- Garlic, (three cloves and minced)
- Hummus (a quarter cup or tahini)
- Lemon (a half medium and juiced—one tablespoon)
- Unsweetened milk or water (to thin)

- Salt for taste

Toppings are optional

- 2 tablespoon lemon juice
- Cherry tomatoes (1/4 cup and diced)
- Chopped parsley(1/4 cups and minced)
- Garlic sauce—chili

Instructions

1. Have your oven heated at 400 degrees then have your baking paper lined using foil.
2. Have your potatoes rinsed and scrubbed then get them to half size. It speeds up your cooking time. Leave them whole as you just bake for the doubled period (forty-five minutes to one hour).
3. Have your chickpeas tossed in oil as well as spices then put your baking paper at the top (foil-lined).
4. Using olive oil get your sweet potatoes rubbed while facing down on your baking paper.
5. As your chickpeas and sweet potatoes roast, make your sauce through putting in all the ingredients in your mixing bowl then combine by whisking; only add adequate amounts of water to the almond milk making it thin thus pourable. Taste and regulate the seasonings as you'd like. Put in more garlic to make zing, some salt as well as citrus juice not forgetting some dill to intensify the herbalflavor.
6. **TIP**: If you're missing hummus, the tahini can make a brilliant base substitution as per the sauce is concerned sauce—just regulate the seasonings conveniently to

accommodate any missing flavor brought out by that tahini.

7. Have your parsley-tomato tossed with citrus fruit and tomatoes to marinate.

8. With your sweet potatoes soft as well as chickpeas browned—about an estimate of 25 min—remove from oven.

9. In terms of serving, turn your potatoes fleshy-side facing up then squash inside a little bit. Have it topped using chickpeas, parsley and sauce.

Nutrition

313 calories, fat 5g, 82mg sodium, 60g carbs,11.7gfibers, 3.9g sugars, 8.6g proteins

WEDNESDAY

Breakfast

Fava Beans and Pita Bread (warm)

Preparation Time of ten minutes, Cooking Time of fifteen minutes

Four serving

Ingredients

- 1 large tomato, diced
- Olive oil (one to one and a half tablespoon)
- Onion (one large and chopped)
- One teaspoon ground cumin
- Parsley (a quarter cup fresh and chopped)
- Garlic (one clove and crushed)
- Red pepper (crushed and in flakes)
- Pita bread (four whole grain) pockets
- One 15-ounce can fava beans
- Lemon juice (a quarter cup)
- Pepper and Salt

Procedure

1. Have your oil heated over moderate to high temperatures for thirty seconds in your skillet.
2. Put in tomato, onion, garlic then have them sauté for three minutes till tender. Put in fava beans as well as its liquid then boil.

3. Put in the cumin, lemon juice and parsley after you've reduced the temperatures then using pepper and salt season for taste.
4. With moderate temperature, have it cooked for five minutes.
5. As it goes on get your pita heated in a pan in moderate temperatures till lukewarm for one to two minutes each part.
6. Dish your meal and serve.

Nutrition

Fat 7g, cholesterol 0mg, calories 325, sodium 831mg, carbohydrate 56g, protein 13g

Lunch

Roasted Tomato Chickpea Soup

Warm healthy soup for that cold day

Cooking Time of twenty minutes

Servings—8

Components

- Oil—olive (2 tablespoons)
- Onion (half a cup and chopped)
- Pepper and salt (a dash)
- Pepper flakes (chili) and garlic powder ½ teaspoon
- ½ teaspoon turmeric
- Paprika (a half teaspoon)
- Lemon (juice from one half)
- Tomatoes (28 oz fire roasted and canned)
- Chickpeas (one can rinse and drained)
- Coconut water (one can)
- Vegetable broth (one cup)
- Parsley—fresh (garnishing purposes) (not a must)
- Sour cream (vegan and dollop) (not a must)

Procedure

1. Have your oil heated in a saucepan, put in your onions then shortly cook till it is brown.
2. Put all your spices, juice (lemon) then have them cooked for a little while.
3. Put in your tomatoes (roasted) then let the get cooked in about 10 mins.

4. Put in Egyptian pea, coconut water, as well as the broth then have it cooked for five minutes.
5. Move your chowder and blend it till it becomes fine. The soup being too thick you may add more broth.
6. Top it with sour cream and parsley.

Nutrition

237.2 calories, 139g fat, 22.3g carbs, 5.5g fiber, 3.2g proteins

Dinner

Chicken (Honey Lime) with Veggies in Foil

Want a clean kitchen?

Preparation Time of fifteen minutes, Cooking Time of fifteen minutes and full time of thirty minutes

4 servings

Components

- Garlic (two cloves and minced)
- Ginger (one tablespoon and minced)
- Unsalted butter (three tablespoon and melted)
- Olive oil—extra virgin (two tablespoons)
- 1 teaspoon cumin
- ½ teaspoon smoked paprika
- 2 tablespoons honey
- Zest of 1 lime
- Black pepper (ground freshly) and salt (kosher)
- Corn (two ears and in halves)
- Cilantro (two tablespoons fresh and chopped)
- Chicken breasts (four 6-ounce)
- Cumin (one teaspoon)
- Paprika (a half teaspoon smoked)
- Asparagus (one bunch)
- ¼ cup thinly sliced green onion

Instruction

1. Stir your butter in a container together with oil honey, lemon zest, ginger, and garlic.
2. Using your 12-inch foil sheet, put up four packets. Have your chicken at the center then have it seasoned using

paprika and cumin. Get your packets with equal asparagus. Have your chicken and asparagus brushed with your previously made mixture then season it using pepper and salt. Get your foil folded on your food then seal by crimping severally.

3. Have your grill heated at moderate temperatures, for thorough cooking grill your packets in ten to twelve minutes.

4. Cook your corn using your grill for five minutes till browned on every part.

5. Before you serve your meal, have the chicken garnished using green onions and cilantro.

Nutrition

474 calories, 29g fat, 24g carbs, 32g protein, 13g sugars

THURSDAY

Breakfast

Lemon Scones

That bittersweet you'll crave with some coffee!

Preparation Time of fifteen minutes, Cooking Time of fifteen minutes

Twelve   servings

Ingredients

- Salt (a half teaspoon)
- Butter (a quarter cup)
- Flour(two cups and a quarter cup)
- Sugar (two tablespoons)
- Baking soda (a half teaspoon)
- Lemon zest (one)
- Buttermilk (three-quarter cup reduced fat)
- Sugar (one cup and powdered)
- Lemon juice (one to two teaspoons)

Instructions

1. Have the oven heated at 400 degrees. Get your salt, sugar, baking soda, and two cups flour combined in a container.
2. For your mixture to resemble fine crumbs use a food processor to get you utter cut in till it shows the results
3. Put in the buttermilk and zest (lemon) and mix by stirring.
4. Turn your dough in a floured out surface kneading six times gently then have your dough in a ball shape and flatten to a half inch thick rounds using a pin (rolling).
5. Have your wedges cut from the circle then get the wedges in three small wedges to give out twelve scones.
6. Put your scones on a baking paper and let them cook for twelve to fifteen minutes.
7. Inside your container make a thin frost by mixing lemon juice and sugar (powdered) on your hot scones pour the frosting before serving.

Nutrition

Fat 4g, Cholesterol 11mg, Calories 175, Sodium 190mg, Carbohydrate 31g, Protein 3g.

Lunch

Harissa Potato Salad

We love this spicy twist on a classic.

4-6 servings

Preparation Time of ten minutes, Cooking Time of fifteen minutes and full time of twenty-five minutes

Components

- Salt (a quarter teaspoon)
- Pepper (a quarter teaspoon)
- One and a half lbs baby potatoes (with the skins on)
- 2 tablespoons harissa paste
- 6 ounces low-fat or non-fat Greek yogurt
- Lemon (one and juiced)
- Cilantro (a quarter cup and fresh), parsley (chopped roughly)
- Red onion (a quarter cup in dices)

Instructions

1. Have your potatoes inside the pot then submerge with one to two inches of salty cold water. Boil your water in moderate temperatures. Proceed to cook potatoes without covering, till they become fork tender, at about 9 to 11 minutes. Drain your potatoes thereafter put them aside.
2. On the other side whisk your harissa, lemon juice, Greek yoghurt, pepper, and salt in a container.
3. Move your warm potatoes onto another container. Put your dressing, fold gently till they are properly

coated(potatoes). Then get your herbs and onion (diced) folded in carefully.

4. Have it served when warm, at room temperature or after being chilled.

Dinner

Salmon Tacos (Healthy Baked)

Some piece of mouthwatering pastry?

Preparation Time of ten minutes, Cooking Time of fifteen minutes and full time of twenty-five minutes

8 servings

Components

- Oil—olive (one teaspoon)
- Tortillas—corn (eight to ten)
- Salmon (one piece and fresh) (a half a pound)
- Chili powder (optional) to taste
- Salt & pepper
- Garlic—powder
- Cumin (grounded)

Sauce:

- Greek yogurt (one cup and plain)
- Lime (a half and juiced)
- Garlic (one clove and minced)
- Cilantro (a handful fresh and chopped)

Topping:

- Avocado (one and in dices)
- Lettuce—iceberg (shredded)
- Wedges—lime for taste

Procedure

1. Have your oven heated at 375F. With the rack placed at the center, get your baking paper lined using a foil.

Have your tortillas wrapped into the foil and placed into your oven.

2. Get your salmon piece on the baking paper then make sure to coat with oil (olive). Softly sprinkle using garlic powder ,chili powder, ground cumin, as well as pepper with salt. Have it cooked in your oven for ten to fifteen minutes or till it easily flakes using a fork.

3. On the other hand, have the sauce components combined as well as the lettuce and avocado prepared

4. Bisect your salmon when ready to small edible sized using a fork. Serve your dish with lime after the tacos are assembled.

FRIDAY

Breakfast

Zucchini with Frittata—Goat Cheese

Preparation Time of thirty minutes, Cooking Time of twenty minutes

Four serving

Ingredients

- Salt (a quarter teaspoon)
- Pepper (an eighth teaspoon)
- Zucchinis (two mediums)
- Eight eggs
- Milk (two tablespoons)
- Olive oil (one tablespoon)
- Garlic (one clove and crushed)
- Goat cheese (two ounces and crumbled)

Instructions

1. Have your oven heated at 350 degrees.
2. Get your zucchinis in a quarter inch thick sliced(rounded). Whisk your pepper, salt, milk, and eggs in a container.
3. Using moderate temperatures get your oil heated in a skillet.
4. Put in garlic and let it cook in thirty seconds. Put in the zucchini then for five more minutes cook.
5. Stir for one minute and our the eggs.

6. Have it topped with cheese and moved to your oven. Get them baked for ten to fifteen minutes. Afterwards, take out the pan from oven and keep aside for three minutes.
7. Using a cutting board, slice your frittata to pie wedges (four) then serve while still hot.

Nutrition

Cholesterol 11mg, 134calories, 324mg sodium, 8g fats, 4g carbs, 12g proteins

Lunch

Greek Salad (Fattoush)

Food for the gods!

Preparation Time of fifteen minutes, Cooking Time of fifteen minutes and full time of thirty minutes

Four to six servings

Components

Salad:

- Wheat pitas (two and whole)
- Red onion(a half small sliced thinly)
- Parsley leaves—Italian (a half cup and flat)
- Feta cheese (three-quarter cup and crumbled)

Dressing:
- Olive oil (a third cup)
- Olive oil (two tablespoons)
- Salt (a quarter teaspoon)
- Romaine lettuce (four cups and chopped)
- Cucumber (one medium sliced, quartered and peeled)
- Bell pepper (one yellow and in three quarter inch pieces)
- Cherry tomatoes (a half pint-one cup and in halves)
- Kalamata olives (a half cup and in halves)
- Vinegar—red wine (two tablespoons)
- Garlic (one small clove and minced)
- Oregano (a half teaspoon and dried)
- Salt (a quarter teaspoon)
- Black pepper (an eighth ground freshly)

Procedure

1. Have your oven heated at 350°F.
2. With the pitas half cut, put them on the baking paper. While baking turn at least once so that you have it browned as well as toast for ten to fifteen minutes. Allow to cool. Get the pitas into edible sizes by cutting then drizzle with two tablespoon oil over your bread. Coat by tossing then sprinkle some salt then distribute well by tossing. Seclude.
3. Inside your container, put in olives, parsley, tomatoes, onions, cucumber, bell pepper, and lettuce and then toss.
4. Vinaigrette—put in a third cup oil, oregano, vinegar, pepper, salt and garlic in a container and blend properly by whisking.
5. Put in your pita pieces as well as feta in your salad then using vinaigrette drizzle on top. Combine it by tossing carefully. Afterwards, serve.

Dinner

Guacamole Quinoa Salad

Something out of the ordinary

Preparation Time of ten minutes, Cooking Time of twenty minutes and full time of thirty minutes

4 servings

Components

- ½ cup loosely packed chopped fresh cilantro
- lime juice (2tablespoons, and freshly squeezed)
- 1 cup quinoa, rinsed
- 2 avocados, halved and pitted
- Onion (a half small diced finely)
- Olive oil (extra virgin), just for drizzling
- Minced garlic, Romaine lettuce, red-pepper (flakes), hot sauce as well as lime wedges, fit for serving
- ½ teaspoon kosher salt
- Black beans (one 15-ounce canned, rinsed and drained)
- Cherry tomatoes (one cup and quartered)

Instructions

1. Cook up the quinoa as per the package's descriptions. Leave it at room temperature.
2. Score the avocado's flesh using a knife; thereafter scoop it into a bowl (large). Coarsely mash the half of avocados using a fork, keep in mind to leave the chunks intact. Mix up in your onion, the cilantro, salt, and lime juice.
3. Have the quinoa, black beans, and tomatoes gently folded in. Taste and adjust the seasonings if desired and have it drizzled using oil.
4. Get it served on your romaine greens bed topped with garlic, hot sauce, and red-pepper flakes alongside lime wedges.

Nutrition

57g carbs, 15g protein, 431 calories, 18g fat, 3g sugars

SATURDAY

Breakfast

Vegetable Omelet

Preparation Time of fifteen minutes, Cooking Time of twenty-five minutes

Four serving

Ingredients

- Pepper (a half teaspoon)
- Goat cheese (a half cup and crumbled)
- Dill (two tablespoons fresh and chopped), parsley, or basil
- Artichoke hearts (a quarter cup, water marinated, rinsed, drained and chopped)
- Olive oil (one tablespoon)
- Six eggs
- Salt (a half teaspoon)
- Fennel bulb (two cups sliced thinly and fresh)
- Roma tomato (one and in dices)
- Green olives (brine-cured) (a quarter cup pitted and chopped)

Instructions

1. Have your oven heated at 325 degrees. Get your oil heated in moderate to high temperatures inside a skillet.
2. Put in your fennel then have it sauté in five minutes till tender.

3. Place in your tomatoes artichoke hearts and olives then sauté in three minutes till tender.
4. Get your eggs whisked in a container then have them seasoned using pepper and salt.
5. Put your eggs in a saucepan with the veggies then have them stirred for two minutes.
6. Using cheese sprinkle on your omelet then have it baked for five minutes till ready.
7. Get them topped using basil, dill or even parsley.
8. Take your omelet out of the saucepan and place on a preferred cutting board. Slice it forming wedges (four).

Nutrition

Cholesterol 13mg, Sodium 496mg, Calories 152, Fat 10g, Carbohydrate 6g, Protein 11g

Lunch

Greek Lemon Chicken Soup

A perfect warmth mixture.

Ingredients

- Onion (one and in dices)
- Carrots (three peeled and in dices)
- Olive oil (2tablespoon and divided)
- Chicken thighs(1 pound of boneless skinless)
- Black pepper (freshly ground) and kosher salt
- 4 cloves garlic, minced
- Celery, (2 stalks and diced)
- Thyme (a half teaspoon dried)
- Citrus juice (two tablespoons squeezed freshly)
- Parsley leaves (2 tablespoons chopped and fresh)
- Chicken stock (eight cups)
- Two leaves—bay
- Canned cannellini beans (two fifteen and a half ounces drained and rinsed)
- Spinach—baby (four cups)
- Dill (two tablespoons fresh and chopped)

Instructions

1. Heat oil (olive 1 tablespoon) using a stockpot (large) or oven (Dutch) with medium heat. For taste, season the chicken thighs using pepper and some salt. Put in the chicken into stockpot then cook till it turns golden for about two to three minutes; thereafter seclude.

2. Put in your oil (1 tablespoon) in the stockpot. Put in your garlic, some onion, the carrots as well as celery. As youcook, keep stirring it occasionally, till it tenderizes for about 3 to 4 min. Stir in some thyme until it becomes fragrant for about a minute.

3. Have the bay leaves and chicken whisked in. Let it boil then get your cannellini beans and chicken stirred in, stir from time to time till it thickens in ten to fifteen minutes.

4. For two minutes, have your spinach stirred in till it wilts. Get your parsley, dill and citrus juice stirred inside then season using pepper and salt.

Nutrition

2.0gfat(saturated), 72.0g cholesterol, 18.0g carbs, 4.0gfiber, calories 241.0g, Protein 19.0g

Dinner

DIN Lemon Herb Pasta Salad

A perfect cocktail of the Mediterranean ingredients.

Preparation Time of ten minutes, Cooking Time of fifteen minutes and full time of twenty-five minutes

10 servings

Components

Lemon herb dressing

- Parsley (two tablespoons fresh chopped finely)
- Garlic (two teaspoon and minced)
- Oregano (two teaspoon and minced)
- Oil—olive (a third of a cup)
- Citrus juice (two tablespoons squeezed and fresh)
- Vinegar—red wine (two tablespoons)
- Water (two tablespoons)
- Basil (one teaspoon and dried)
- Salt (a half teaspoon)
- Pepper (cracked)

For salad

- 1 avocado, peeled, pitted and chopped
- ½ of a large red pepper deseeded and cut into thin strips
- Cherry/grape tomatoes (nine ounces in halves)
- Lettuce leaves—Romaine (four cups dried, washed)
- Cucumber (one large and in dices)
- Tomatoes—sun-dried (a third cup drained, oil-packed)

- Feta cheese (five to six tablespoon and crumbled)
- Red onion (a half sliced thinly)
- Kalamata olives (a half cup sliced and pitted)

Procedure

1. Have your pasta boiled in a big pot till al dente. Get it drained into a colander maybe or a strainer, thereafter rinse with water (cold) to remove the heat. Transfer your pasta to your mixing bowl (large).
2. While pasta is boiling, prepare your dressing. Using a big jug whisk in all your dressing components.
3. Put your salad components into abowl together as well aspasta, and drizzle with the dressing. Put in all the ingredients combined until everything has evenly coated in the dressing. If you'd like, season with some extra salt as well as pepper.

Nutrition

Sodium 129mg, Potassium 201mg,Calories 108, Saturated Fat 1g,Total Carbohydrates 3g, Dietary Fiber 1g

WEEK 4 DIET PLAN

SUNDAY

Breakfast

Sweet Potatoes Stuffed with Avocado-Tahini and Chickpeas

That extra energy and mouthwatering dish?

Preparation Time 10 minutes, Cooking Time is 40 minutes bringing a total time of 50 minutes

Ingredients

- Lemon zest(one tablespoon)
- Fresh oregano(one tablespoon)

- Marinated chickpeas
- Garbanzo (one 15 oz canned rinsed and drained)
- Pepper (red)(1/2 in dices)
- Oil (olive extra-virgin)(three tablespoons)
- Lemon syrup/juice (one tablespoon)
- Sweet potatoes(8 medium sized and rinsed well)
- Garlic(one clove crushed and a half teaspoon)
- Freshly chopped parsley (one tablespoon)
- Salt (a quarter teaspoon)
- Avocado Tahini Sauce
- Ripe avocado(1 medium sized)
- Toppings
- Tahini (a quarter cup)
- Water(a quarter cup)
- Garlic (one clove mashed)
- Fresh parsley(one tablespoon)
- Fresh lemon juice(1 tablespoon)
- Pumpkin seeds (a quarter cup)
- Either fragmented vegan feta or regular feta-to keep it dairy free

Procedure

1. Have your oven heated at 400°.
2. Pierce using any fork few holes on your sweet potatoes to allow the air to escape. Put them inside your baking pan then for forty-five to sixty minutes have them bake till softening. The larger the sweet potato, the longer it will need to bake fully.
3. While the potatoes are baking, work on the chickpeas. In a bowl (medium sized), combine the chickpeas and the rest of the ingredients needed in marinating. Toss in

the chickpeas until they're all well coated in the marinade then put aside for later.

Avocado Tahini Sauce

➤ In making the sauce, put in every sauce ingredients and blend till it becomes even. Maybe you'd want a thin consistency, put in another 1-2 tablespoons of water. Once it is smooth put the sauce to a small bowl and place aside.

Assembly

➤ Once they are tender(sweet potatoes)to the touch, remove them and let them become cool before handling. When cutting a slit down the middle of every potato,carefully spoon the chickpeas in there. Top it with the avocado tahini and sprinkle up the pepitas on the top with the crumpled up feta. These are best served fresh, but you can keep them refrigerated for two days.

Nutrition

Calories 308, 7g proteins, fat 15g, carbohydrates 38g, 8g fibers, sugar 5g, 307mg sodium

Lunch

Mediterranean Quinoa Bowls

One exotic meal to bring some sweet dreams.

Preparation Time of fifteen minutes, Cooking Time of five minutes

Components

Roasted Red Pepper Sauce:

- Juice of one lemon
- ½ cup olive oil
- Roasted peppers—red, (1 16-ounce jar and drained)
- Garlic(1 clove)
- ½ teaspoon salt
- ½ cup almonds

For that Mediterranean special Bowls

- Kalamata olives
- Pepperoncini
- Cooked quinoa
- Thinly sliced red onion
- Hummus
- Spinach, some kales, or cucumbers
- Feta cheese
- Parsley or fresh basil
- Oil (olive), some lemon juice, some pepper, sea salt

Instructions

1. Pulse the ingredients making the sauce in the food processor as well as a blender till it's mostly smooth. It should be textured and thick.
2. Cook the quinoa as per the package instructions. When it's ready (the quinoa), build that Mediterranean Quinoa meal packed bowl!
3. Have the leftovers stored separately in containers as well as assemble every bowl moments before serving, most likely the greens as well as sauces, because they'll be soggy when put with ever other ingredients.

Dinner

Greek Shrimp Farro Bowls

Cause it's a freaking weekend! Enjoy the veggies.

Preparation Time for 10 minutes, Cooking Time at 20 mins bringing a total time of 30 minutes

4 servings

Components

- Twoteaspoons of fresh chopped dill
- 3 Tablespoon of oil (olive)
- Garlic, (2 cloves and minced)
- A pound of peeled deveined shrimp
- Oregano (one fresh tablespoon and chopped)
- ½ teaspoon paprika(smoked)
- ½ teaspoon salt
- ¼ teaspoons pepper(black)

- 1 lemon juice
- Faro(one cup and dried)
- Bell peppers,(two and thickly sliced)
- Zucchinis,(two medium-sized and sliced to rounds(thinly)
- Cherry tomatoes, (one pint and halved)
- Green or black olives(a quarter sliced thinly)
- plain Greek yogurt(4 tablespoons with 2% reduced fat)

Instructions

1. Put oil (olive), garlic, salt, dill, lemon, paprika, oregano, and some pepper all into your bowl. Combination through whisking. Put in ¾ of your marinade on the shrimpfish then toss it for coating. Allow it's standing for 10 mins.
2. Have the faro cooked as per the specified instructions (in package) either inside the water or in stock.
3. Either have a nonstick skillet heated or a grill pan in some moderate heat (medium). Put in the shrimpfish; cook it for 2-3 mins each side, till it's not pink anymore; move it to your plate.
4. Put in vegetables in form of batches into your skillet or grill (and don't overcrowd); cooking it for 5-6 minutes till it softens. For every other veggie carry out the same.
5. Putthe Farro equally into bowls (4). Evenly have it topped using the shrimpfish, the vegetables (grilled), tomatoes as well as olives. Have the marinade (reserved) drizzled onthe top using a tablespoon top each bowl.

Nutrition

Calories 428,protein 34mg, Saturated fat 2mg, Carbohydrates13.5mg, Fiber 6mg, Sugar 6mg, Sodium 540mg, Cholesterol 174mg

MONDAY

Breakfast

Moroccan Eggs with Tomato Sauce

Preparation Time of fifteen minutes, Cooking Time of thirty minutes and full time of forty-five minutes

Three servings

Components

- Tomato paste (one and a half tablespoon)
- Olive oil (one tablespoon)
- Onion—red and chopped
- Garlic (one clove and grated)
- Paprika (one teaspoon)
- Salt (a quarter teaspoon)
- Pinch of sugar optional
- Tomatoes (one and a half cup and chopped)
- Cumin (a half teaspoon and grounded)
- Black pepper (a half teaspoon)
- Eggs (three and large)
- Cilantro (one tablespoon) or parsley (chopped)

Instructions

The instructions given can be used when cooking with a Moroccan earthen pot or just a regular frying pan.

1. Use a tagine to put the oil (olive), the chopped leeks, the grated garlic together with water(1/4 cup) and have it placed on your heat diffuser which is over the stove using moderate temperatures in approximately ten to fifteen minutes.
2. Put in oil, the garlic, onions or leeks as well as water into the tagine.
3. If you're using some frying pan, heat the oil (olive) then sauté red onions or chopped leeks, grated garlic and about one fourth cup water and let it simmer for about 5 to 10 minutes.
4. Put in the tomato paste, your chopped tomatoes, the spices, pepper, salt, sugar and allow it to simmer about 5 to 10 minutes more.
5. Regulate the sauce's consistency by putting water (1-2 tablespoons) as required, until it resembles pasta sauce (thickness).
6. When you are simmering ensure to put the tagine's lid as supposed to.
7. Crack your eggs in the sauce. Cover your dish with tagine's lid and poach your eggs for 5-6 minutes till they are ready.
8. Using pepper and salt have it seasoned. Get cilantro preferably or the parsley and use as garnish.
9. Transfer the dish to a dry wooden surface.
10. If using a tagine to prepare this dish, remember that the heat coming from the tagine when hot (earthen pot) will continue cooking your eggs even after removing the dish from the stove, so you may turn off the stove and take the dish early before reaching the preferred final consistency of your choice(for the eggs). Leave it for three to five minutes till pleasant as preferred.

11. Serve the Moroccan eggs with tomato sauce and toasted bread preferred by you.

Nutrition

Calories 142, 10g fat, 211mg cholesterol, potassium 375 mg,phosphorus 129mg, 7g carbs, sugars 4g, 2gfibers, 8g proteins

Lunch

Mediterranean Chicken Tacos

Chicken has never tasted any better.

Preparation Time of ten minutes, Cooking Time of twenty minutes and full time of thirty minutes

Eight servings

Components

- Onion (a quarter cup and in slices)
- Feta cheese (two thirds a cup)
- Cucumber (a half a cup)
- Lemon (half a lemon juiced)
- Dill (two teaspoon and fresh)
- Taco shells(eight soft)
- Chicken breasts (two to three thawed edible pieces),
- Grape tomatoes (a half cup and sliced)
- Hummus (one cup)

Tzatziki sauce:
- Garlic (six cloves)
- Mint leaves (two)
- Greek yogurt(a half cup plain)
- Pepper together with salt

Instructions

1. Heat a large skillet with oil (1-2 tablespoons) then cook the chicken in the skillet till ready.
2. While chicken is cooking, make the tzatziki sauce and the hummus. For tzatziki sauce: put together the garlic,

the cucumber, dill, the lemon as well as mint in the blender then pulse for about 5 to10 seconds. Put into a bowl (large) then stir by hand the yoghurt until everything has been combined.

3. Chop the tomatoes as well as onions in the meantime having the chicken cook.

4. Once the chicken is ready, put in the bowl of the sauce (tzatziki) then stir till the chicken has been well coated.

5. Heat the taco shells using a skillet till it's warm then you can fill with hummus, the chicken as well as vegetables.

Dinner

Tabbouleh Salad (Cleansing)

Cleansing your taste buds has never been this enjoyable.

Preparation Time 15,total time 35 minutes

Ingredients

- Sticks (two celery and chopped)
- Onion—red (a half and chopped)
- Cherry tomatoes (one pint and in halves)
- Grain (one and a half cups cooked) (rice-brown/quinoa)
- Cauliflower (half head florets)
- Cucumber—English (a half and chopped)
- Parsley (half cup chopped freshly)
- Hemp hearts (a quarter cup)
- Dressing (oil free)
- Vinegar—red wine (three tablespoons)
- Maple syrup (one tablespoon)
- Pepper and salt
- Water (two tablespoons)
- Lemon (one juiced)
- Garlic (one clove and minced)

Instructions

1. Prepare your brown rice from your choice of grain, as per instructions given.
2. In the food processor, make sure to pulse the cauliflower till grain-like. Move your florets to your container. Put the cucumber, (chopped), celery, the onion, the tomatoes, as well as the hemp hearts and parsley.

3. Combine with the grain of choice (cooked). Make sure to mix properly.
4. With your dressing prepared have it poured on your salad. Combine well by mixing.
5. To combine the flavors, put inside your fridge for several hours or have it served warm.

TUESDAY

Breakfast

Greek Guacamole

For the early riser craving that Mediterranean magic touch.

Preparation Time of 10 minutes ringing a total time of 10 minutes

Components

- Ripe avocados (2 big halved and pit removed)
- 2 tablespoon lemon juice
- 1 heaping tablespoon chopped tomatoes(sun-dried)
- Ripe cherry tomato (3 tablespoons and diced)
- Red onion (¼ cups and diced)
- Oregano (one tablespoon and dried)
- Parsley(twotablespoons chopped and fresh)

- kalamata olives (4 whole ones pitted and chopped—not a must)
- Salt and pepper-black (one pinch)

Instructions

1. Put in avocado together with your lemon juice into a mixing bowl (large) then mix and mash your mixture(use a fork or potato masher).
2. Put in the remaining ingredients (olives are not a must), combine well by stirring. Sample and add salt and pepper if needed.
3. Regulate otherflavors if need be, additional lemon for some acidity, the tomato (sun-dried) for that deeper tomato flavor, onion for crunch/spice, or the parsley or maybe oregano.
4. Immediately enjoy withpita, some pita chips, or even vegetables. Enjoyed when fresh.

Nutrition

110 calories, 6g carbs, 1g sugar, 10g fat, sodium 54mg, protein 1g, 4g fibers

Lunch

Mediterranean Salad with Tomato Vinaigrette (sun-dried)

A quick one to prepare.

Preparation time of ten minutes and full time of ten minutes

Components

Mediterranean Salad

- A third a cup red onion (sliced thinly)
- Half a cup feta cheese (crumbled)
- Grape tomatoes (two cups and halved)
- Cucumber (two cups and chopped)
- Artichoke hearts (one cup and chopped)
- Tomatoes-sun dried (two tablespoonsoil-packed)
- Vinegar-apple cider (four teaspoons)
- Garlic (one clove)

Tomato Vinaigrette (sun-dried) Dressing

- Olive oil (six tablespoons)
- Sea salt (a quarter teaspoon)
- Black pepper (an eighth teaspoon)

Instruction

1. Making the dressing, puree the oil, tomatoes (sun-dried), vinegar (apple cider), the garlic, salt, and black pepper until it's smooth as well as emulsified. (If it's thick, try thinning out using more water or oil, as well as puree again.)
2. Combine the tomatoes, cucumbers, artichokes, onions, feta in a big container. Using the dressing toss it.

Nutrition

Calories 155, Fat 12g, Protein 4g, Total Carbs 9g, Net Carbs 7g, Fiber 2g, Sugar 5g

Dinner

Shrimp with Cauliflower "Grits" and Arugula.

Those Mediterranean veggies always stand out.

Preparation Time of five minutes, Cooking Time of twenty-five minutes and full time of thirty minutes

4 servings

Components

Spicy Shrimp

- Garlic (two teaspoons powdered)
- Shrimp(one pound deveined and peeled)
- Paprika (one tablespoon)
- Olive oil—extra virgin (one tablespoon)
- Cayenne pepper (half teaspoon)
- Black pepper(ground freshly) and salt

Cauliflower Grits

- Whole milk (one cup)
- Goat cheese (half cup and crumbled)
- Butter-unsweetened (one tablespoon)
- Cauliflower (four cups and riced)
- Black pepper (ground freshly) and salt

Garlic Arugula

- Garlic (three cloves sliced thinly)
- Baby arugula (four cups)
- Olive oil—extra virgin (one tablespoon)
- Black pepper (ground freshly) and salt

Instructions

1. Make the Spicy Shrimp: Put the shrimp inside a bag (zip-top, plastic). In a bowl, have your paprika stirred with powdered garlic as well as the cayenne for combining. Have the mixture in the bag having the shrimps and toss till well they are coated in spices. Refrigerate while you make the grits.

2. Making Cauliflower "Grits": Melt your butter in moderate temperatures inside your pot. Put your cauliflower rice thereafter cook till it moisture is released, about two to three minutes.

3. Have half your milk stirred in and simmered. Let it simmer, stirring occasionally until the cauliflower absorbs some of the milk, 6 to 8 minutes.

4. Put in milk (remainder) and have it simmer till the mixture thickens and becomes creamier, about 10 minutes more. Have the goat meat stirred and seasoned with some salt as well as pepper.

5. Make the Garlic Arugula: Into a skillet (large), have your oil heated in moderate temperatures. Put in garlic then have it sauté till fragrant, 1 minute. Put in the arugula as well as sauté till wilted, about 3-4 minutes. Get it seasoned using pepper and salt, take out of your skillet and seclude.

6. Get your oil heated over moderate temperatures in the same skillet. Put in your shrimp as well as the sauté till cooked properly, in four to five minutes. Get it seasoned using pepper and salt.

7. For serving, divide your grits among plates (4) topping each with arugula (1/4) as well as (¼) shrimp.

Nutrition

Spicy Shrimp

122 calories, 16g protein, 5g fat, 3g carbs, 0g sugars

Cauliflower Grits

151 calories, 8g protein, 5g sugars, 10g fat, 9g carbs

Garlic Arugula

35 calories, 0g protein, 3g fat, 1g carbs, 0g sugars

WEDNESDAY

Breakfast

Foster (Banana) and Streusel-Cinnamon (Toppings)

Preparation Time of six minutes, Cooking Time of two minutes

2 servings

A healthy yet delicious meal

Ingredients

- Cinnamon (half teaspoon and separated)
- Coconut oil—virgin (two teaspoons)
- Walnuts (a quarter cup)
- Flaxseed meal (two tablespoons grounded)
- Brown sugar (three teaspoons and separated)
- Bananas (two peeled and sliced to a quarter inch rounds)
- Greek yogurt (one cup and plain)

Instructions

1. Streusel: have the brown sugar, flax meal, cinnamon and walnuts combined into a food mixer. For the walnuts to be chopped finely, get the ingredients pulsed together. Then seclude.
2. Bananas: Get your oil (coconut) heated in your sauté pan thereafter put in bananas (sliced) where you'll cook with moderate temperatures for one minute. Get your bananas sprinkled using cinnamon as well as sugar, have low temperatures and cooka minute more.

3. For every serving, have Greek yogurt (half cup) inside your container, topped using bananas as well as a mixture of cinnamon streusel.

Nutrition

Calories 355kcal, carbohydrates 40g, protein 15g, 17g fat, 5mg cholesterol, potassium 684m, fiber 6g, sugar 23g

Lunch

Mediterranean Pasta Salad

A cool refreshing salad

Preparation Time of twenty minutes, Cooking Time of ten minutes and a full time of thirty minutes

Six servings

Components

- Garlic (one teaspoon powdered)
- Onion (a half teaspoon powder)
- Sea salt (a teaspoon)
- Pepper(fresh and cracked)
- Red pepper—Chile (a half teaspoon and crushed)
- Extra firm tofu (one block)
- Fusilli pasta 16-ounce dried
- Red onion (a half a mug and in dices)
- Cucumber(one large one in dices)
- Grape tomatoes(one pint and halved)
- Kalamata olives (a half cup)
- Artichoke hearts (1 14-ounce canned) drained, quartered and rinsed
- Basil (a quarter cup and chopped)
- Citrus juice(two to three tablespoons and fresh)
- Pine nuts (a quarter cup)
- Olive oil—extra virgin (a third mug)
- Vinegar—red wine(a quarter cup)
- Mustard (one and a half tablespoon)
- Maple syrup (one and a half teaspoons)
- Oregano (two to three teaspoons and dried)

Instructions

1. Place your pasta into a pot (large) of boiling water (salted). Cook it till firm but soft as per the package's instructions (approximately nine to ten minutes). Using cold water, rinse to stop it from cooking further then drain before secluding.

2. Whisk every dressing ingredients in a bowl. Regulate flavors where necessary. It might come out kind of saltish, remember it spreads across your pasta.

3. Have your tofu (crumbled) sprinkled with salt, and then on top put one to two tablespoons of the marinade. To properly coat, work it gently using your fingers. For tangier flavor, put little amounts of citrus juice. Place secluded.

4. Put in pasta, the pepper(onion),olives, tomato, cucumber, artichokes as well as your basil. Have the dressing poured on everything and slowly combine by tossing. Now put in your tofu gently as well as tossing again. Discern by tasting a little for the dressing then regulate where necessary.

5. Have your bowl covered and refrigerated in two to three hours to allow marinating of flavors. Cover bowl. When finished, top with pine nuts. As well you could put in the vegan parmesan, some pepper (freshly-cracked) at the top.

Dinner

Lebanese Lemon Chicken

Healthy and extremely flavorful

Preparation Time of five minutes, Cooking Time of twenty-five minutes and a full time of thirty minutes

Serves six to eight

Components

- Sea salt (one and a half teaspoon and flaky)
- Black pepper (ground freshly)
- Lemons (three and organic)
- Olive oil—extra virgin(two tablespoons), extra for cooking
- Turmeric (a half teaspoon and ground)
- Chicken thighs (three pounds skinless and boneless)(twelve pieces)
- Two scallions(large) or onion(one and large)
- Thyme (two sprouts and fresh)
- Rosemary (two sprouts and fresh)

Procedure

1. Blend a lemon till you have lemon juice (2 tablespoons). Put juice into a bowl (large), put olive oil (2

tablespoons) with your turmeric, the salt, and black pepper(freshly ground).

2. Put in your chicken thighs in a bowl and coat it by tossing. Allow your poultry to souse shortly in normal temperatures as your components are being prepared.

3. Shave off the two citrus fruits then slice to rounds (thick) (1/4 inch). Take out the seen seeds. Peel, cut into a half as well as cut your scallions.

4. Have you (2) skillet heated with moderate temperatures. Put in enough oil for coating of the bottom.

5. Divide your chicken pieces into pans (2) having the chicken's smooth side down, ensure to have very small spaces in the middle of your chicken to allow browning. Have them cooked in five minutes till the bottom is finely brown. For the second side, have it flipped and cooked for eight to ten minutes, till it cooks well, check to keep your temperatures slightly low if needed. Take a plate and put your chicken pieces in.

6. Inside your pans have the citrus fruit, herb sprout as well as a scallion. Let cook undisturbed for 3-4 minutes, till the lemons become brown at the bottom. With water (1/2 cup) poured and stirred into each pan and, scrap any brown substance at the bottom. Having your moderate temperature put back in your chicken in your skillet then have it cooked for four to five minutes for flavors to meld. Serve your meal when hot over some rice or maybe cauliflower rice.

THURSDAY

Breakfast

Waffled Falafel

Ingredients

- 3 garlic cloves
- ½ teaspoon ground coriander
- Garbanzo beans (three cups and cooked and drained)
- Olive oil—drizzle pump
- Cilantro (a quarter cup and chopped)
- Onion (one small and chopped)
- ½ teaspoon ground cumin powder
- Beetroot (one and large)
- An avocado
- Garlic (one clove and peeled)
- Salt to taste
- Flour(a third garbanzo floor)—besan
- Baking soda (a teaspoon)
- Beetroot relish
- Salt
- ½ lime juice

Instructions

1. For falafel, have a food mixer for blending garbanzo, the parsley (Chinese), onion, powder (coriander), the cumin seeds, the salt, lime juice (lemon) as well as garlic for taste till there isn't any big chunk.
2. Put garbanzo (bean flour) as well as baking soda.
3. Transfer this mixture to a large bowl.

4. As it sets up, have your beetroot a bit relish. Mix a big beetroot, avocado (1), garlic clove (1), lime juice (1/2) with some salt for taste in the processor till the texture is creamy.

5. As per manufacturer's instructions, heat the waffle maker as well as spray oil and have medium temperatures. Spoon the falafel (mixture 1/3 cups) in every cavity and have it closed. Cook for about 10 minutes, till it's crispy and browned lightly.

6. In the bowl with cucumbers (chopped) get your waffle (falafel) arranged in as well as the chopped cucumber, avocado, corn kernels, the cabbage/lettuce then serve together with the beetroot relish.

Lunch

Fresh and Easy Tuna Salad (Nicoise)

Simple yet classy.

Prep Time of ten minutes, Cooking Time of twenty minutes and full time of thirty minutes

Four servings

Components

Vinaigrette:

- 6 tablespoons olive oil
- ¼ teaspoon salt
- Dash of pepper
- Vinegar—red wine (two tablespoons)
- Garlic (one teaspoon fresh and minced)

For the Salads:

- Salt (a half teaspoon and divided)
- New potatoes 12 ounces
- ¼ teaspoon garlic powder
- Eggs (four, hard-boiled and sliced)
- Olives (twenty whole and pitted)
- Anchovy fillets 1.2 ounce
- Olive oil (two tablespoons and separated)
- Green beans (twelve ounces fresh and trimmed)
- Greens (salad) (six cups)
- Cherry tomatoes (one cup)
- Tuna fish 2, 4.5 ounces
- Parsley(a quarter cup fresh and chopped)

Instructions

Vinaigrette:

1. Put your ingredients in a sealable jar and shake to combine. Roast the veggies
2. Have your oven at 200°C. Using a cooking spray line your big baking paper then put aside.
3. In hand, have a plastic bag (zip-top and large) and put your potatoes in. Putolive oil, the garlic powder as well as salt. And gently toss for potatoes to evenly coat in the seasonings and oil.
4. Spread the potatoes on the baking sheet. Having to stir only once get your potatoes to roast for fifteen minutes.
5. In the meantime, have your green beans inside a plastic bag (zip-top and sizeable). Put in a tablespoon of oil in that bag, together with a quarter teaspoon salt. In order to coat your beans in salt and the oil, have it tossed.
6. Having roasted in about 15 mins, take out and spread your beans on the paper having potatoes in one layer.
7. Have your green beans and potatoes back to the oven to be roasted approximately ten to fifteen minutes or till they become tender. Very small potatoes are ready in 20 minutes as big potatoes need thirty minutes. Ensure they are soft inside and crispy outside.

The Salads:

1. Divide the greens (lettuce) among bowls (serving) evenly.
2. Top every lettuce bowl with the tomatoes, eggs (boiled), the olives, the anchovies, the tuna, the roasted potatoes as well as green beans. Have some vinaigrette and garnish drizzled on together with parsley.

Nutrition

Calories 574.7, 42.3g fats, 7.2g fats (saturated), 224.8mg cholesterol, 1159.6mg sodium, carbs 24.2g, fibers 6.3g, 5.3g sugars, 26g proteins

Dinner

Mediterranean Couscous with Tuna and Pepperoncini

Preparation time 3 minutes, Cook 12 minutes = Total 15 minutes

4 servings

<u>Ingredients</u>

Couscous

- 1¼ cups couscous
- A cup of water or chicken broth
- ¾ teaspoon kosher salt

Accompaniments

- 1-pint cherry tomatoes, in half
- 1 lemon quartered

- ½ cup sliced pepperoncini
- ⅓ cup chopped fresh parsley
- Two 5-ounce cans of oil packed tuna
- ¼ cup capers
- Salt (Koshar) and black pepper (ground freshly)
- virgin olive oil

Instructions

1. How to make Couscous: boil your broth or water in heat (medium). Remove the pot from heat, stir your couscous and put a lid on it. Leave forat least 10 minutes.
2. Make the Accompaniments: in a bowl put in together the tuna, tomatoes, pepperoncini, parsley, and capers.
3. Fluff the couscous with a fork, season with the salt as well as pepper, and then drizzle with oil (olive). Top your couscous with using tuna mixture then serve with lemon wedges.

Nutrition

Couscous

226 calories, 1g fat, 44g carbs, 8g protein, 1g sugars

Accompaniments

193 calories, 9g fat, 6g carbs, 22g protein, 3g sugars

FRIDAY

Breakfast

Almond Raspberry Banana Baked Rice

Components

- Brown rice (one cup and cooked)
- Honey (one tablespoon)
- Lemon zest (one tablespoon)
- 2 bananas, sliced
- ½ pint raspberries
- 4 tablespoons slivered blanched almonds

Instruction

1. Have your oven at 375°. In the covereddish, put in rice, the banana slices, as well as 2 tablespoons of almonds. Softly fold in raspberries, and then drizzle with honey. Top it with the remaining almonds as well as lemon zest, afterwards drizzle with honey. Bake for about 20 minutes.

Nutrition

Calories 180, Fats 4.5g, Saturated fat 0g, Proteins 4g, Carbohydrates 35g, Sugar 13g, Fiber 6g

Lunch

Easy Turkish Red Lentil Soup Recipe

Servings—2-3

Prep Time of ten minutes, Cooking Time of twenty minutes and a full time of thirty minutes

Components

The Soup:

- 1 tomato cut small
- One carrot
- Red split lentils (20grams)
- Olive oil (one to two tablespoons)
- Onion (one and sliced)
- Garlic (two cloves)
- Lemon juice (onetablespoon)
- Black pepper ¼ teaspoon
- Salt to taste
- 1 teaspoon paprika
- ½ teaspoon cumin
- Tomato paste 1 tablespoon
- Broth (200ml)

To garnish:

- Olive oil
- Chilipowder or flakes
- Fresh peppermint

Instructions

1. Before you start cooking, I hope that you will keep the red split lentils for 20-30 mins soak. This will soften lentils— that will cook faster. Same time makes sure the lentils remain soft.
2. Prepare all your vegetables before you start out cooking. This will help your cooking flow.
3. To start cooking, put the oil-olive into a pan then fry the onion slices till soft. Continue adding the tomato with the garlic and with carrot pieces.
4. Then season with the paprika and the cumin powder and tomato paste. Stir and fry content with low to medium heat.
5. At such a point, then you may put in the lentils (strained) and the broth. After properly mixing allow ten to fifteen minutes of simmering. Your pot will be full of the lentils as well as they'll be soft.
6. Blend the entire soup to be smooth without any pieces or bits. Return to heat if it gets cold(soup). Then as you have removed it from the heat source, pour in juice (lemon) and mix in.
7. Have your soup in a bowl then have it garnished using drops of oil (olive), the chili pepper as well as the fresh peppermint.

Nutrition

Calories 424kcal,fat 12.34g, sodium 1500mg, fiber10.8g, fat (saturated) 7.24g, fat 10g(unsaturated),

carbs 59.17g, sugars 7.24g, fibers 10.8g,23.3g proteins, 10mg cholesterol.

Dinner

Creamy Mediterranean Chicken

5 servings

<u>*Ingredients*</u>

- Chicken breasts(1½ lb.), pound to ½ inch thick
- Oil (2 tablespoons)
- Minced garlic (1teaspoon)
- 1¼ cups half-and-half cream
- Artichoke hearts, (one 14-ounce dressed, drained and canned)
- ¼ cup julienne cut sun dried tomatoes
- ⅓ cup kalamataolives pitted
- ¼ cup Parmesan cheese
- ¼ cup feta cheese
- Basil (two tablespoons sliced and fresh)

<u>*Procedure*</u>

1. In moderate temperature, have your oil heated on your skillet.
2. Using pepper and salt, season your chicken then put inside your pan. For four to five minutes, have it cooked till browned then flip. Cook until internal temperature is 165 then remove chicken from skillet.
3. In your skillet, put in the garlic and have it cooked for approximately thirty seconds as you constantly stir. Put in cream, artichoke; the tomatoes-sun dried and the olives. Low boil and it then cook it while stirring till slightly thick.

Stir cheese (Parmesan) cheese and put in your chicken inside your cooking pan. With your heat off, garnish with feta and basil.

Nutrition

Fat 6g, cholesterol 60mg, fiber 5g, sodium 272mg, fat 14g, potassium 463mg

SATURDAY

Breakfast

Cinnamon Toast Waffles with Pomegranate Syrup (orange)

Preparation Time of ten minutes and Cooking Time of thirty minutes bringing a full time of forty minutes

Servings (four)

Ingredients

- Spiced pomegranate orange syrup
- ½ teaspoon ground cinnamon
- Orange juice (two mugs)
- Pomegranate juice (a single cup)
- Coconut oil (one tablespoon)
- Salt (an eighth)
- ¼ teaspoon ginger (grounded)
- Cardamom (an eighth and grounded)

Gluten-Free Waffles

- 2 cups 3-ingredient gluten-free flour(all purpose)
- Salt (a half teaspoon)
- Cane sugar (a tablespoon)
- Baking powder (two teaspoons)
- 1½ cups milk
- A teaspoon cinnamon
- Two eggs (large)
- Butter (a quarter mug and melted)
- ½ cup slivered almonds
- ½ teaspoon pure vanilla extract

- Additional Ingredients
- 1 cup pomegranate arils

Instructions

1. Make the syrup
    Pour the orange and the pomegranate juices into a saucepan then boil it by heating. To gently boil, reduce your temperatures then cook until juices have reduced and thicken. With heat reduced have your salt stirred in, coconut oil as well as the spices. Bring the heat to medium and continue cooking, this allows syrup to thicken. Take off your skillet from the heat source, and let it cool.
2. Make the waffles
    Heat waffle iron. Combine the salt, sugar, baking powder, cinnamon, and flour into your container. Combine your ingredients by stirring properly. Put in the eggs, butter, milk as well as vanilla into your ingredients (dry ones), whisking them till ingredients have been combined properly. Pour the batter into your waffle iron (hot), and cook as per manufacturer's instructions.
3. Arrange the waffles
    Toast the almonds in your pan with medium heat, stir frequently, in approximately five minutes till a light brownish (golden) color. Take out your almonds immediately preventing further cooking. Split into 4 portions, then top waffles with pomegranate(1/4syrup) and toasted almonds(2 tablespoons) and 1/4 cup of the pomegranate arils.

Nutrition

Calories 318, fiber 5g, sugar 17g, carbohydrates 42g,potassium 463mg, protein 8g

Lunch

Greek Salad with Chickpeas

Prep Time of10 mins and full Cook Time of 10 mins

Components

- Cucumber (one hothouse and cut to bite-able pieces)
- 1 teaspoon dried oregano
- Four tomatoes (Roma and in dices)
- 1 small red onion thinly sliced
- 1 red bell pepper, in dices
- ¼ cup extra virgin
- Bell pepper,(one yellow and in dices)
- Kalamata olives (one cup pitted and drained)
- Vinegar—(red wine) (three tablespoons)
- Chickpeas (one 15oz canned rinsed and drained)
- 1 cup fresh herbs
- Pepper(ground freshly) and salt (for tasting)

Procedure

1. Start by combining your cucumber, herbs, onions, tomatoes, peppers, olives, and chickpeas.
2. Have your oregano, vinegar as well as oil (olive), then dress using the Greek dressing, combine by tossing evenly.

Nutrition value

Calories 172, protein 4g, 15g fiber,total fat 11g, sodium 294mg,transfat(2g),cholesterol 9g,carbohydrates 6g, 4g sugar

Dinner

Mediterranean Cobb Salad

For that colorful plate.

2 servings

Preparation ten minutes, full time of ten minutes

Ingredients

Salad

- Four cups lettuce(Romaine)
- ½ cup kalamata olives
- 1 to 2 hardboiled eggs, thinly sliced
- 1 cup marinated roasted red peppers, drained
- ¾ cup English cucumbers, diced into small pieces
- 2 cups—artichoke hearts
- ¾ cup feta cheese, crumbled or diced small
- About 2 tablespoons fresh basil, for garnishing

Vinaigrette

- ½ teaspoon dried dill
- Vinegar—(red wine) (one to two tablespoons)
- ½ teaspoon dried basil
- 1 tablespoon honey, or to taste
- Oregano (a half teaspoon and dried)
- Salt (a half teaspoon)
- 3 to 4 tablespoons olive oil

- Black pepper (a half teaspoon and ground freshly)

Procedure

1. Salad—evenly scatter the Romaine and lay down the remaining ingredients in long rows, and evenly sprinkle with fresh basil then set aside.
2. Vinaigrette—To a container put all ingredients, shake vigorously to evenly combine, taste vinaigrette and make any adjustments (if needed), evenly drizzle over salad and enjoy when fresh.

Life After the Four-Week Meal Plan and Habits to Keep the Diet

After your weeks with these diverse choices of meals, you'll obviously have a liking for some and come out with several favorite dishes. Well,it's expected. What do you expect from the Mediterranean if not pure bliss? To maintain the lifestyle after getting used to the timetable is not difficult because what you have to do is just continue or restart afresh, this time reshuffling diets, some of the tips recommended, however, are:

- Continue enjoying your favorites—it's not the end of the beautiful appetizing meals.You still have the meal plan with you, so redo and redo once more. If it made you feel good and healthy—an obvious fact, then feel free.

- Focus on your satisfaction—if there's a meal that made you full and you loved it, stack up on it. At the end of the day, the calculated nutrients are still the same and are improving your health.

- Repeat the meal plan all over—having being used to a timetable, having random meals in an untimely fashion will only lead you south real quick. You can shuffle the diets in terms of days and times and see how it goes. Get adventurous and have fun!

CHAPTER 3: FITNESS EXERCISE WITH BODY MANAGEMENT

Exercise, undoubtedly, is essential to all people to enhance fitness and healthy life. People control their weights in many ways, with this being one of them. Exercise helps one to keep their numbers on the scale reasonable and within normal health parameters. Exercise is good for every individual to keep healthy and fit. Without this, one would end up with lifestyle diseases or even become obese. In this day and with cars and improved modes of transport, people no longer sort after walking. Well, your muscles become stagnant, weak, and inactive or even disabled in one way or another. With the presence of processed and chemicalized foods, it's best to regularly exercise and balance calorie levels in your body. There are various types of exercises which will fit everyone's preference and liking. This is because not everyone is capable to lift weights or do much tougher modes of exercise. Again, technology has provided all that is needed to undertake such activities, so you have no excuse to not exercise. The various ways of exercising include:

- Yoga
- Weight training
- Aerobics

Benefits of Physical Exercise

- Improve one's health
- Reduces chances of getting chronic illnesses
- Strengthens one's immunity
- Improves self-confidence as well as moods

- Improves one physical state—strength and muscle build

Tips for Successful Weight Control and Physical Exercise

- Have a systematic formula—Have more activities into your day and plan them out wisely considering your schedules. Don't go about with random decisions or unplanned activities that will later cause you inconvenience.
- Have a goal in mind—You are not just in the gym to pass time. Plan out your end goal and work towards it, be it muscle gains or weight loss, have something to work on. In the meantime, you could have short-term goals in the process to mark progress and to motivate you more.
- Have a support system—This is something you can't do on your own. Seek guidance, advice from your folks, trainer or even spouse for encouragement as well. This will help you see that you're not in this alone. This journey will not be easy, but with the right support system, you'll thrive and come out successful.
- Be adventurous—Don't always go for the aerobics, and you perfectly know you're past that stage. Explore new grounds, try something new, something to get you out of your comfort zone; new milestones, and at the end of it all, you'll come out curved out for success.
- Consult your body—How? Well, our body function is different, and one thing that's working for someone else's might not work for you. So, listen to what your body is saying (reactions) and implement.

- Eat healthily—You can't be on a health journey with terrible meal choices. Gas up on that healthy and have a variety of foods to sample as well as help you keep fit.
- Mark progress—Always mark out the times you conquer a milestone. This motivates you to see that there is progress as well as brings you closer to your main goal.
- With regular fitness activities, your life will improve; you'll feel good, look better, and even enjoy the process. Regardless of whether your main aim is to cut on your wait or just be physically fit being physically engaged will lead you to that healthy lifestyle.

CHAPTER 4: SHOPPING LIST

As the shortest part of this guide, well, it's quite simple and self-explanatory on what it entails. A shopping list is what you go with to the stores tobuy stuff. Primarily, it contains some of the things you're buying, at what quantities and at what price. In a meal plan, this is very essential, and you have seen in the previous chapters how it comes in handy. You may be wondering about how you can shop and still remain on a budget? Well just hang on there; the following are ways you can shop within a budget.

- Go on a strict budget/list and stick to it, don't compromise.
- Plan your meals beforehand so that you get to gauge your expenditure.
- Visit the store countless times rather only go when necessary.
- Don't involve your emotions when shopping, buy needs, not wants
- Always go for the economy packs—things to last you for a longer time.
- Conduct price checks beforehand to have an evaluation of your expenditure.
- Always have a calculator or somewhere to do your numbers, to make sure you don't exceed your estimates or parameters
- Buy only what you can afford, it's that simple

A Shopping List of Things You Might Need on That Mediterranean Diet

- Grains—Whole grain bread, pasta, cereals

- Vegetables and fruits—Guacamole, bananas, lemon, banana, oranges, apples, berries etc. Kales, spinach, cabbage, lettuce, garlic, onions, tomatoes, etc.
- Legumes—Black beans, peas, beans, lentils
- Nuts—Almonds, groundnuts, cashew nuts
- Tubers—Sweet potatoes, potatoes,
- Condiments—salt, black pepper, turmeric, garlic, cinnamon, etc.
- Meat/fish/poultry—lean red meat, Salmon, sardines, turkey, trout, chicken, eggs.
- Dairy products—milk, cheese, cream, Greek yogurt.
- Oils—coconut oil, olive oil.

For healthy meals, as per the recipes given, stock up on those ingredients and have your own five-star restaurant at the heart of your home—kitchen.

Conclusion

If you're reading this, you've been able to go through the whole book. It's an honor to have you take your time and go through this guide. This shows your devotion and interest in a healthy lifestyle as well as nutritional principles. The main drive behind this book's existence is to show and bring the light to you, the reader, as well as point out and illuminate the way for you in this journey. I hope that it has been of great help as well as become a reference point for informative health matters.

Now, with the knowledge at hand, you have no excuse but to seize the opportunities life has presented to you to change and take or continue on that journey to wellness. This is only a guide that points out various ways, and it does not confine you only to the information it relays. Go all out and do your research as well as consult and try out different and new ideas. Let this book catapult you to the next pedestal in health matters as well as personal wellness.

With discipline and sheer determination, this book is just one of the many arrows in your quiver of riches. With gradual progress, aiming for success using this arrow does not assure you of victory, but it is on how you use it and strategize on how to execute your plans. So, **if you've found this book helpful in any way, a review on Amazon is very much appreciated.**

Made in the USA
Columbia, SC
11 June 2019